IMAGES OF ENGLAND

CATHOLICS IN BIRMINGHAM

IMAGES OF ENGLAND

CATHOLICS IN BIRMINGHAM

CHRISTINE WARD-PENNY

TEMPUS

Frontispiece: Stained glass window in St Edward's Chapel showing Archbishop Ilsley leading a procession of St Chad's relics 1919. Window by Donald Taunton; photograph by Jonathan Mahoney.

First published 2004

Tempus Publishing Limited
The Mill, Brimscombe Port,
Stroud, Gloucestershire, GL5 2QG
www.tempus-publishing.com

British Library Cataloguing in Publication Data.
A catalogue record for this book is available from the British Library.

ISBN 0 7524 3362 8

Typesetting and origination by Tempus Publishing Limited.
Printed in Great Britain.

Contents

Foreword

The growth of the Catholic community in Birmingham during the nineteenth and twentieth centuries is a remarkable story. When St Peter's church was opened off Broad Street in 1786 there were less than 500 Catholics in the city. By 1841 there were sufficient to warrant the building of St Chad's Cathedral. In 1850, Birmingham became a diocese and Bishop William Bernard Ullathorne OSB spent the thirty-eight years of his episcopate overseeing a constant expansion with the building of churches, convents and schools. The result is a rich heritage of Catholic faith and life across the city and indeed the whole region.

I warmly welcome this new book which records and celebrates something of our history and traditions. We are proud of our contribution to the city and this book will help to open it up to a wider public. There is much to appreciate, to enjoy and to learn from it for everyone.

Revd Brian Doolan
Dean of St Chad's Cathedral

Acknowledgements

The help of the following is gratefully acknowledged: colleagues at the Central Library, especially Maggie Hanson, Peter Drake and Joe McKenna, Fr Brian Doolan, Dean of St Chad's Cathedral and President of the Archdiocesan Historical Commission, Revd Dr John Sharp, Archdiocesan Archivist, Sister Hilary of St Paul's Convent, Selly Park, Mike Byrne of Acocks Green Library, Mr Michael Hodgetts, Fr Gregory Winterton of the Oratory and Jonathan Mahoney. The following have generously permitted use of their images in addition to the above: the Birmingham Oratory, Birmingham Central Library, the Sisters of the Charity of St Paul, the head teachers of St Paul's Girls School, Archbishop Ilsley Catholic Technology College and Sixth Form Centre, the Oratory School, Father Hudson's Homes Society and the individuals who have lent family photographs.

Introduction

This book of photographs is an attempt to capture the flavour of what Roman Catholics have brought to and fostered in Birmingham. I have tried to open a window into a tradition which has made a major impact on the city, from early martyrs to archbishops, from men of letters to craftsmen and social pioneers. The majority come from the city's own central library but previously unpublished material from other sources is included.

Birmingham's first church was described in the Domesday Book, St Peter and St Paul's at Aston, with another, St Martin's, built shortly after the Norman Conquest on the site of its present-day namesake in the Bull Ring. By 1560 eleven out of twelve people were Catholics. Christianity had come to the Midlands in AD 653 when four monks from Lindisfarne accompanied the newly baptised King Paeda of Mercia home. One, Diuma, became the first bishop, but it was the fifth bishop, Chad, 'the apostle of the midlands' who is best remembered for his missionary zeal and saintliness, with his relics eventually being translated to the new Catholic Cathedral of St Chad consecrated in Birmingham's Gun Quarter in 1841. Once, in what is now Old Square, stood the Austin friars' Priory of St Thomas the Apostle, built around 1250, with a hospital and a chapel dedicated to St Thomas of Canterbury nearby. Stones from the priory were unearthed during the building of the Minories in 1892, and parts of medieval wall-paintings and painted roof-beams were discovered in St Martin's during the rebuilding of 1852, offering us a tantalising glimpse of the first church: '... the priests in their vestments, the lighted candles on the altar, the clouds of incense rising in the chancel, the gleam of colour from wall and window and roof and floor, with the great picture of the Last Judgment above the chancel arch. Medieval St Martin's was a church not unworthy of a town destined to become one of the greatest communities in the kingdom, and one to which Birmingham may look back with pride.' (*History of Old St Martin's* by Bunce, mid-nineteenth century)

With the Dissolution of the Monasteries and the Reformation, all but two Catholic churches disappeared. The Elizabethan Penal Laws after the Act of Uniformity in 1559 heavily fined recusants, non-attenders at Church of England services, then, in an atmosphere of political frenzy between the Armada and the Gunpowder Plot, branded Catholic priests as traitors, to be hunted down and executed along with those who had harboured them. The small town of Bermyngcham set in farmland and heath probably saw many of these brave priests ghosting through to the manor houses and farms which hid them in priest-holes and secret chapels while they sustained and reclaimed the faithful. Their names echo down the centuries in the names of modern Birmingham schools; Humphrey Middlemore, St Edmund Campion, St Ambrose Barlow, St John Fisher, St John Wall. Andrew Bromwych of Oscott, sentenced to death before the feared Sir William Scroggs, was released after imprisonment to his house, now Maryvale. Even after persecution ended, discrimination remained, and when a new church and convent was built at Masshouse Circus in 1687, it was burned down by a mob a year later. Edgbaston housed a Franciscan Masshouse and school but Catholics kept a very low profile and there was no formal hierarchy: the region was overseen by a Vicar-Apostolic. To be Catholic was to be different.

The Murphy Riots showed that people in Birmingham felt the same public wariness about popish influence from overseas, savagely expressed in *Punch* cartoons, although the Catholic Relief Act of 1791 and the Catholic Emancipation Act of 1829 officially removed political and religious discrimination. Catholic converts still faced social ostracism from former friends and were barred from some Government and University posts for a while after this.

Birmingham boomed in the industrialised age of the nineteenth century, growing in prosperity and taking in a huge influx of desperately poor Irish Catholics with a critical need for churches, educational facilities and welfare. Somehow the Birmingham Catholic population found the money and manpower not just to provide, but to lead, with the seminary at Oscott and the intellectual gifts of John Henry Newman at the Oratory on Hagley Road augmenting the number of educated and politically influential Catholics in the area. The resources came from the people themselves: schools and charities had to be financed almost entirely by subscription, and sacrificial giving by the poorest or the youngest, such as the children's pennies for Father Hudson's Homes, played as big a part as philanthropic donations. The Earl of Shrewsbury was a major patron of A.W. Pugin, a convert, and the Catholic Hardmans, father and son, adorned the cathedral. Missions were established in every area of Birmingham, often starting with a corrugated iron church or assembly hall followed by a brick building with a school attached. And what did it matter if your chalice was pewter if it had been designed by Pugin? The best craftsmen in England allied artistry with mass production and both were from Birmingham.

The consecration of St Chad's Cathedral in 1841 meant that the religious importance of Birmingham to the diocese grew in conjunction with the growth of the City of Birmingham in the region. When the official Church structure was restored in 1850, Birmingham's Vicar-Apostolic became a diocesan bishop and under the energy and vision of leaders such as Bishops Walsh, Ullathorne and Ilsley, the spiritual and social outreach of the Church expanded to meet the need. Social conditions created by poverty, disease, drink and further waves of refugees attracted religious orders back from the Continent such as the Sisters of Mercy or the Sisters of Charity of St Paul at Selly Park who founded St Paul's Girls School and nursed sick children at St Gerard's Hospital, Coleshill, famously refusing to turn the hospital over to the War Department but taking in the soldiers as well as the children. In 1911 the diocese became an archdiocese and as Victorian principles of self-help gave way to the Welfare State for all, the financial burdens eased.

Birmingham today is a multiculturally diverse city where religious tolerance has replaced discrimination and every faith can feel at home. There are tens of thousands of Roman Catholics in the city, many from other countries, and when Pope John Paul II came as a welcome guest to the Midlands in May 1982, Birmingham turned out in force to greet him. This book is dedicated to the present day Catholics of Birmingham from an Anglican fellow-traveller, with the greatest of respect.

one

Echoes of the Past

Chad B C

True to Celtic tradition St Chad travelled long distances on foot, until compelled by Archbishop Theodore to ride on horseback. It is said that Theodore lifted the reluctant saint onto the horse himself. This is a tile from the presbytery at Lichfield Cathedral.

Right: Stained glass window from St Edward's chapel, St Chad's Cathedral, showing Canon Arthur Dudley gathering up the relics of St Chad in haste in 1538 when Henry VIII's soldiers arrived to destroy the shrine.

Opposite: A statue of St Chad in the Cathedral in mitre and cope, holding a model of Lichfield Cathedral in his right hand. After his death from plague in AD 672 he was buried beside his cathedral of St Mary, but later reburied in the new church of St Peter consecrated in Lichfield in AD 700.

Left: Second light showing Arthur Dudley taking the relics into hiding. They can be traced to High Arcal in Staffordshire after which they were lost for some years until they were rediscovered underneath an altar near Aston in 1840 by Fr Benjamin Hulme.

Below: High Arcal, Staffordshire, home of the Hodgetts family where the relics are said to have been secreted in the tester of a four-poster bed.

Opposite: Part of a medieval wall-painting and painted beam discovered at St Martin's church in the Bull Ring when the parish church was rebuilt in the 1850s. The painting shows St Martin on horse-back and the beam from the arch above the chancel is from a scene of the Last Judgement. The display in St Martin's in the Bull Ring also contains monuments of the de Bermingham family from the original church founded here in the twelfth century.

Remains of Sandwell Abbey, Handsworth, *c.* 1890. The Prior locked himself in when the abbey was raided by a lawless member of the de Parles family, Sir William de Parles in 1254. The priory lands started on the left of Park Lane.

Remains of St Thomas' Priory discovered underneath the Minories in the middle of the city centre in the 1890s. The Austin friars built a priory and also a hospital dedicated to St Thomas the Apostle around 1150 where Old Square and the Priory Shopping Centre now stand.

The chapel of Deritend 1375-1737 reputed to have been built so that people did not get their feet wet travelling to Aston!

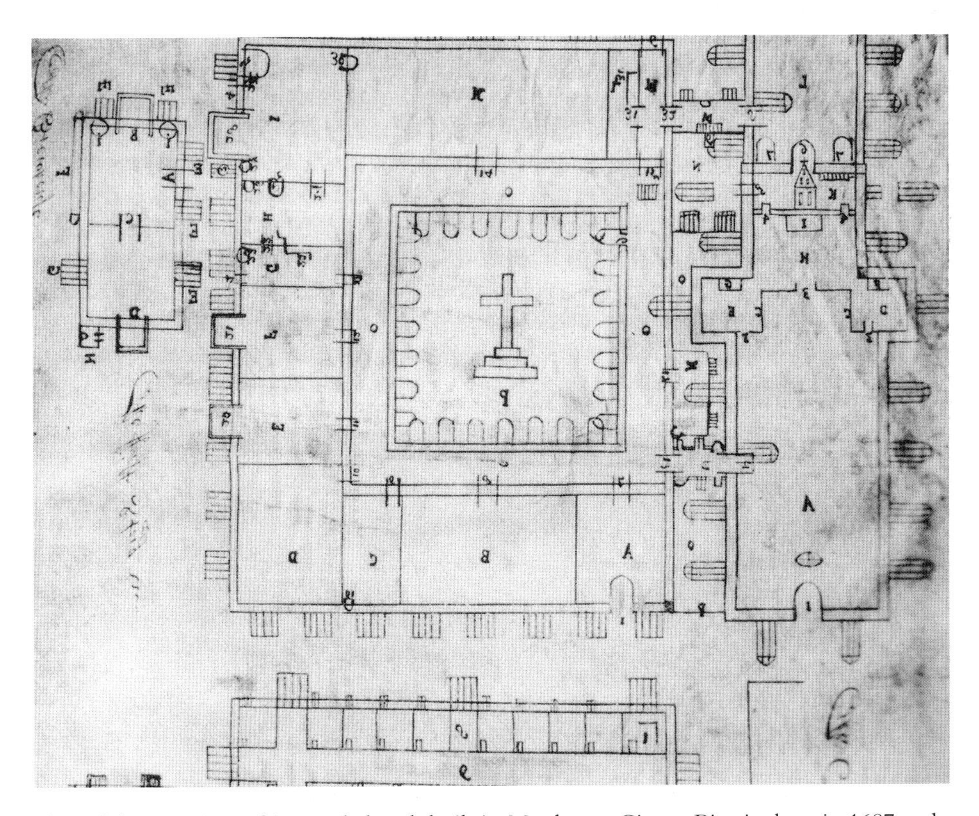

Plan of the Franciscan friary and church built in Masshouse Circus, Birmingham in 1687 and burned down by a mob a year later, from an original copy in the Archdiocesan archives.

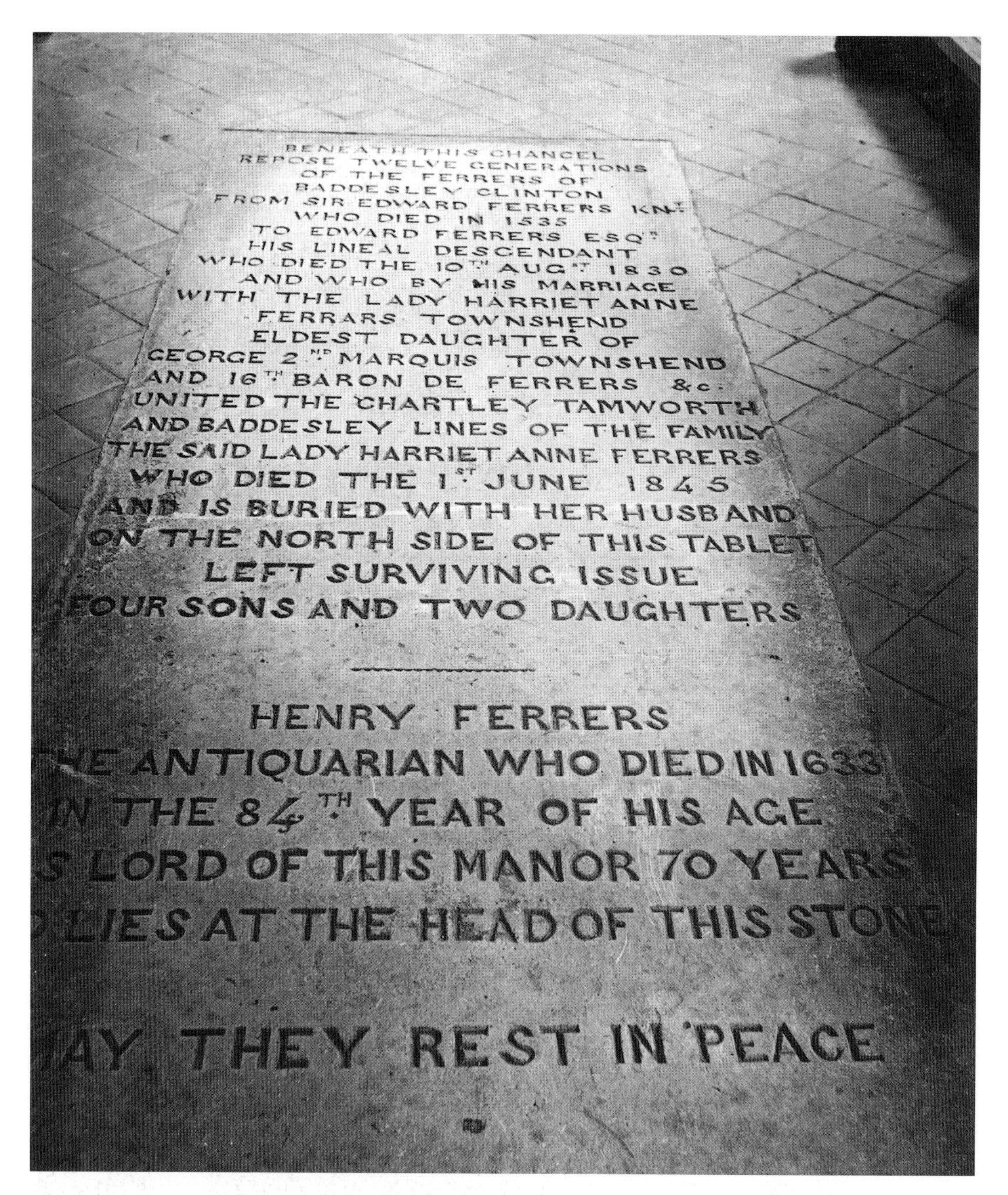

The Ferrers' vault in the church at Baddesley Clinton. After the Reformation Catholics could not officially be buried in Anglican churchyards but in practice recusant gentry were still interred in family vaults and commemorated by memorials in parish churches. The Ferrers were a notable Catholic family who owned Baddesley Clinton Hall. Lesser mortals would be buried in the churchyard at night with a blind eye turned by the authorities. Baptisms and marriages were often performed by both rites to guarantee legitimacy.

Right: In 1919 Archbishop Ilsley reinstituted the annual Procession of the Relics of St Chad around the city. The relics were removed from their seventeenth century reliquary above the High Altar in 1996 and scientifically examined. Five of the six bones fit the history of St Chad and the Archbishop of Birmingham issued a decree authorising the continued cult of the relics but specifying that veneration should only be given to all the relics together so that one particular bone cannot be isolated from the others.

Below: Procession of the relics of St Chad, 25 May 1919, attended by a lay guard of honour.

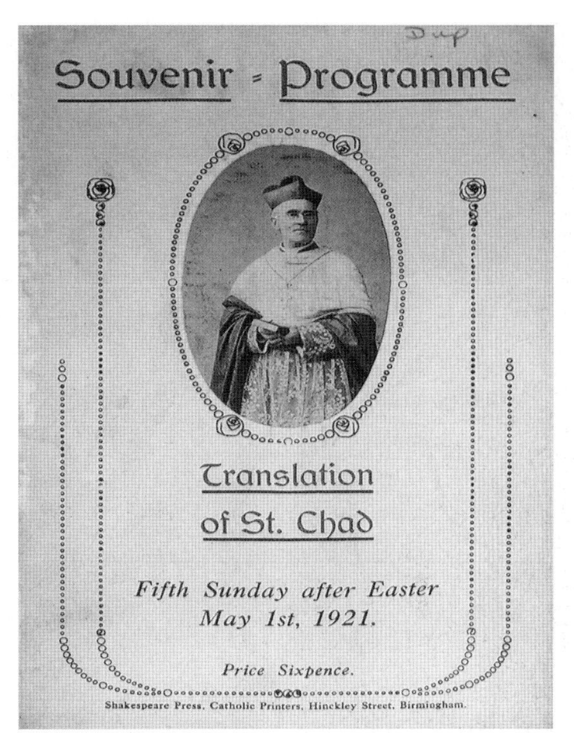

Souvenir - Programme

Translation of St. Chad

Fifth Sunday after Easter
May 1st, 1921.

Price Sixpence.

Shakespeare Press, Catholic Printers, Hinckley Street, Birmingham.

Above: Annual procession, *c.* 1930. Birmingham Catholics processed in parishes, led by their parish priest, but later correspondence in the archive shows that it was a men-only affair by then. In 1965 a group of Anglicans from St Chad's London took part.

Right: Annual Procession, 6 March 2004 following the Mass of St Chad. Among the guests was the Dean of Lichfield Cathedral, Michael Yorke. The casket containing the relics is a new one made for them after their examination in 1996. The seventeenth-century reliquary is now in Oscott College museum.

By 1839 Birmingham's Catholic population had outgrown the chapel in Shadwell Street and Bishop Walsh commissioned A.W. Pugin to design a cathedral 'worthy of the metropolis of the Midland district'. St Chad's Cathedral was consecrated in 1841 and originally it had only one spire as this 1853 engraving shows, the second being added in 1856. In 1933 St Edward's Chapel was added, an original part of Pugin's plan, omitted for lack of funds, and alterations to the roof and floor were made in 1967 when the rood screen was removed and a new high altar facing the people was added.

Interior of St Chad's Cathedral, *c.* 1853. The interior was richly decorated and furnished due to the generosity of Lord Shrewsbury, the Hardmans and Pugin himself. The pulpit, Bishop's throne and canons' stalls are all Flemish work of the fifteenth century as is the statue of Our Lady. John Hardman gave the rood screen, high altar and loft. Altogether the Cathedral cost £20,000 of which Bishop Walsh gave £14,000 from a legacy.

Above: Side view of St Chad's, *c.*1920. Later the rebuilding of the area isolated it on St Chad's Queensway, the major ring road of the 1970s.

Left: St Anne's, Alcester Street, 24 March 2004. Archbishop Vernon Nichols celebrates the Vigil Mass of the Annunciation with priests from the Deanery. This was the first time the relics of St Chad had been displayed in a parish. The Venerable John Henry Cardinal Newman's red biretta is pictured on the table in front of the casket. Cardinal Newman served the area when he opened the first Birmingham Oratory in Alcester Street. Also in the picture are Canon Pat Browne, Episcopal Vicar for Birmingham, Fr Brian Doolan, Dean of the Cathedral, and Fr John Carlyle, Diocesan Treasurer. (courtesy *Birmingham Catholic News,* Easter 2004)

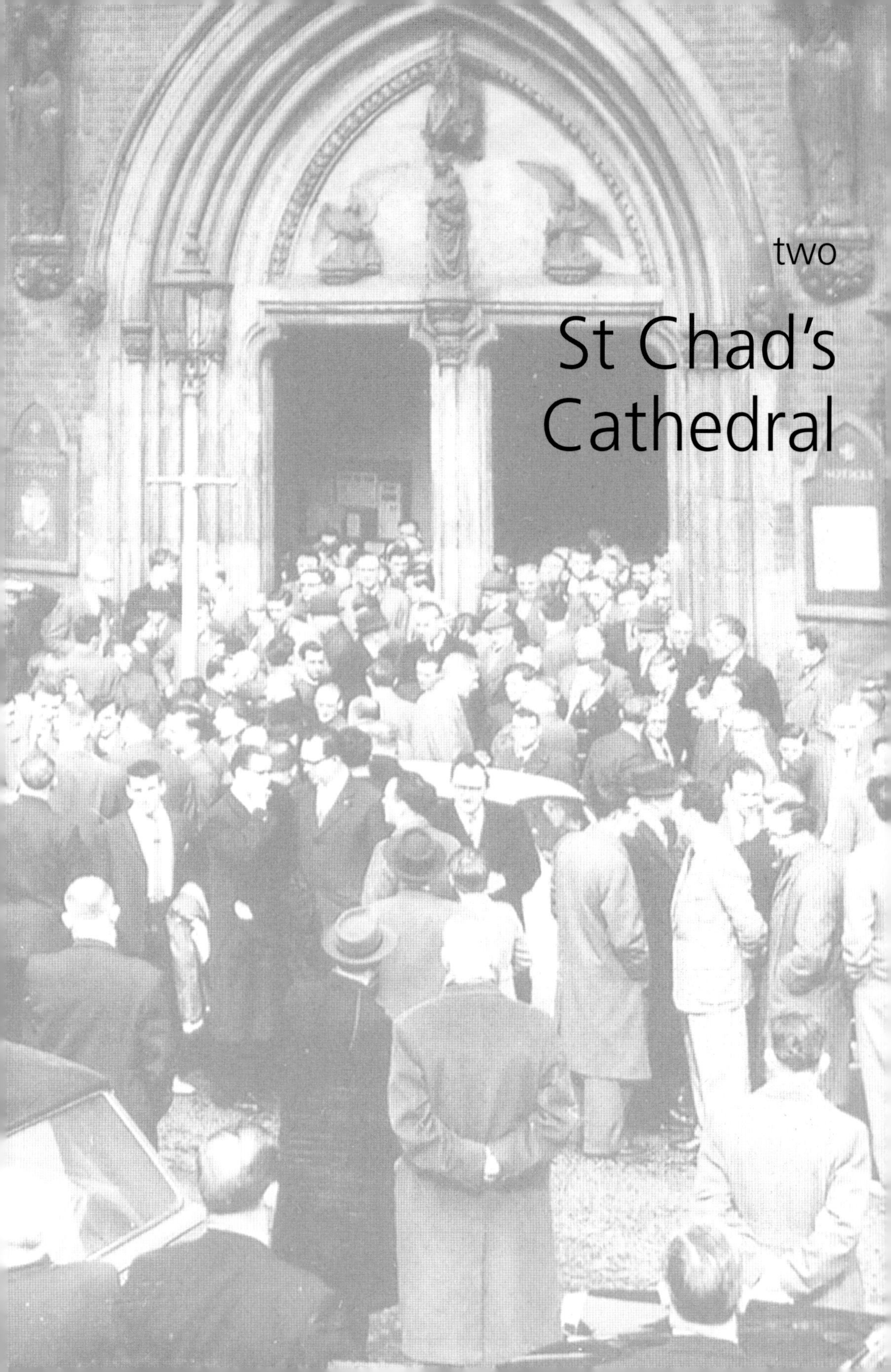

two

St Chad's Cathedral

Above: Outside the Lady Chapel, *c.* 1902. The fifteenth century statue of Our Lady was donated by Pugin in 1841. To the left is the founder, Bishop Walsh's monument. The Lady Chapel itself was stencilled in blue and gold and the side-window, just visible, shows the Annunciation with figures of boys and girls as a reminder that it was given by children of St Chad's schools in 1844. An elaborate oak screen divides the aisle from the Lady Chapel.

Opposite: St Chad's Cathedral 1902, view from the west end looking down the nave. From the main doors, the pillars screen minor areas so that the attention is directed to the high altar and the soaring height of the building which is basically a single hall. In this photograph the original tiled floor and rood screen are shown – both were to go in the redecoration of 1967.

Left: Altar, Lady Chapel, 2004. On the front are stone carvings of the Presentation in the Temple; the Nativity and the Adoration of the Wise Men. Above the altar are Our Lady, the Annunciation and the Visitation. The overall effect of gold and blue is to illuminate this part of the cathedral.

Below: Carved rood screen by A.W. Pugin given by the Earl of Shrewsbury but dismantled in 1967 and rescued from a builder's yard to adorn Holy Trinity church in Reading.

Left: Ordination ceremony, 1960. Men about to be priested give themselves in their entirety to the service of God before the new high altar at St Chad's, which contains relics of the martyrs Clement and Severus. Pugin's old high altar is set against the wall behind it, with the casket containing the relics of St Chad suspended below.

Right: Holy Oils in the Chapel of Chrisms, used to anoint Catholics during baptism, ordination and in the shadow of death.

St Chad's Cathedral, 2004. (Photograph by J. Mahoney)

Left: Archbishop Francis Grimshaw (episcopate 1954-1965) distributing blessed palms, Palm Sunday 1961. Others pictured are Fr Harrington, Very Revd B. Withers and Fr. Kenny, the Archbishop's secretary.

Below: Maundy Thursday, 1960.

Right: The wedding of Alfred and Gertrude Goodby at St Chad's, Whit Monday, 1921.

Below: Requiem for Pope Pius XII, 1959. Archbishop Grimshaw is in reflective mood with Canon John Roskell.

The funeral procession of Archbishop Williams (episcopate 1929-46), 1946. Pictured are Cardinal Griffin, the Duke of Norfolk, Lord Stafford (in Army uniform) Mgr Emery (Rector of Oscott College) and Mgr Collingwood (far right).

Girl Guides welcoming Archbishop Dwyer (episcopate 1965-82) to Cathedral House. This is the new Cathedral House.

The old Archbishop's House, St Chad's, Bath Street, now demolished.

The fifteenth-century Flemish pulpit originally in the church of St Gertrude in Louvain now in St Chad's. It has four carved black oak panels depicting St Jerome, who translated the Bible into Latin in the fourth century; St Gregory the Great, who sent the first missionaries to Kent in AD 597; St Augustine of Hippo and St Ambrose.

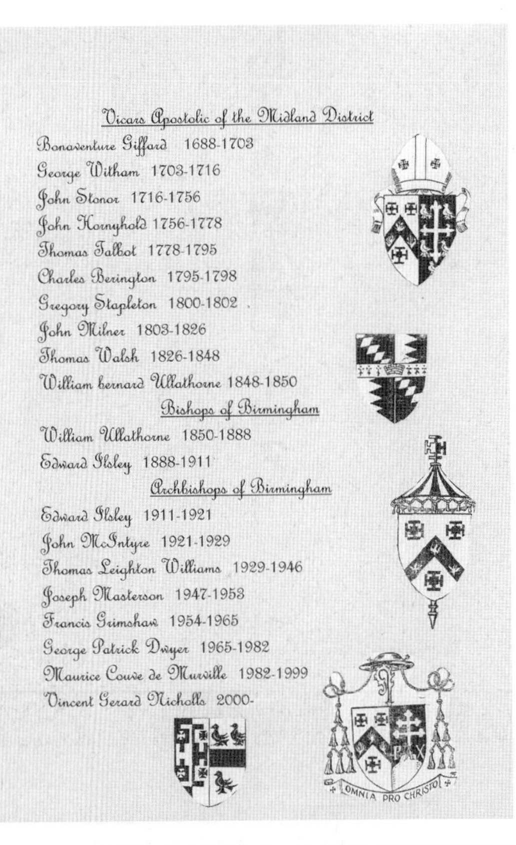

Vicars Apostolic, Bishops and Archbishops of St Chad's 1688-2004. The coats of arms are, from top down, Arms of the Most Revd Edward Ilsley, first Archbishop of Birmingham 1888-1911, Arms of the City of Birmingham 1889-1977, Arms of the Metropolitan Cathedral of St Chad, Arms of the Rt Revd William Bernard Ullathorne, OSB, first RC Bishop of Birmingham 1850-88, Arms of the Rt Revd Thomas Walsh, Vicar Apostolic of the Midland District (from *The Heraldry of St Chad's* by Redman).

Bishop Walsh's Monument, designed by Pugin and made by George Myers was shown at the Great Exhibition of 1851 where Queen Victoria famously asked who Dr Walsh was. Bishop Thomas Walsh was President of Oscott College, Vicar Apostolic of the Midland District 1826-40 and of the new Central District 1840-47. A legacy enabled him to largely fund the building of St Chad's Cathedral, a model of which he is shown holding in his right hand. A firm supporter of Pugin's ideas, he promoted the Gothic revival in architecture, liturgy and vestments throughout the diocese.

Above: The congregation leaving Mass at St Chad's, *c.* 1965. There are now tens of thousands of Catholics in the City of Birmingham.

Right: The spires of St Chad's rising behind the mural in memory of the charismatic Catholic President John F. Kennedy in St Chad's underpass; 'There are no white or coloured signs on the graveyards of battle.' The diocese has Irish, Polish and Vietnamese chaplaincies.

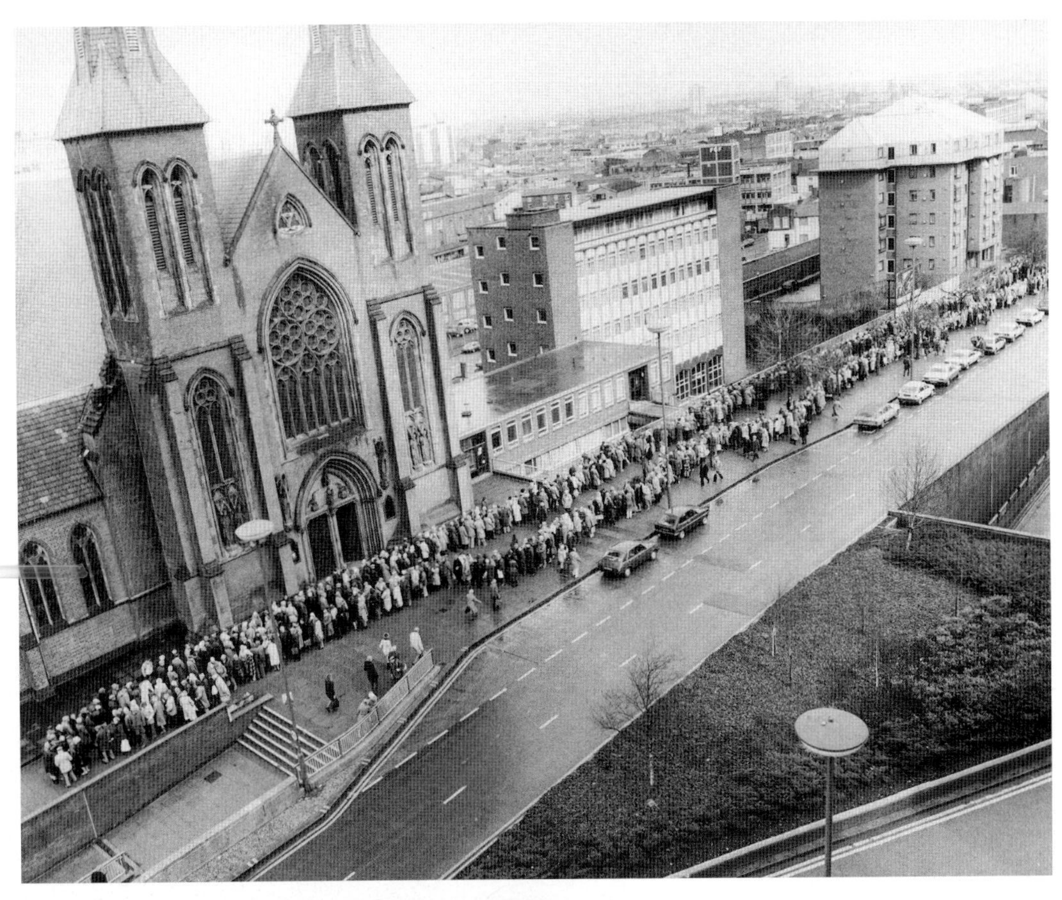

Above: St Chad's may be physically isolated from the rest of the city by the concrete collar of the ring road but Catholics are no longer isolated in society.

Left: Mgr John Roskill on the twenty-fifth jubilee of his priesthood. The monstrance was made from gold contributed by the congregation and melted down.

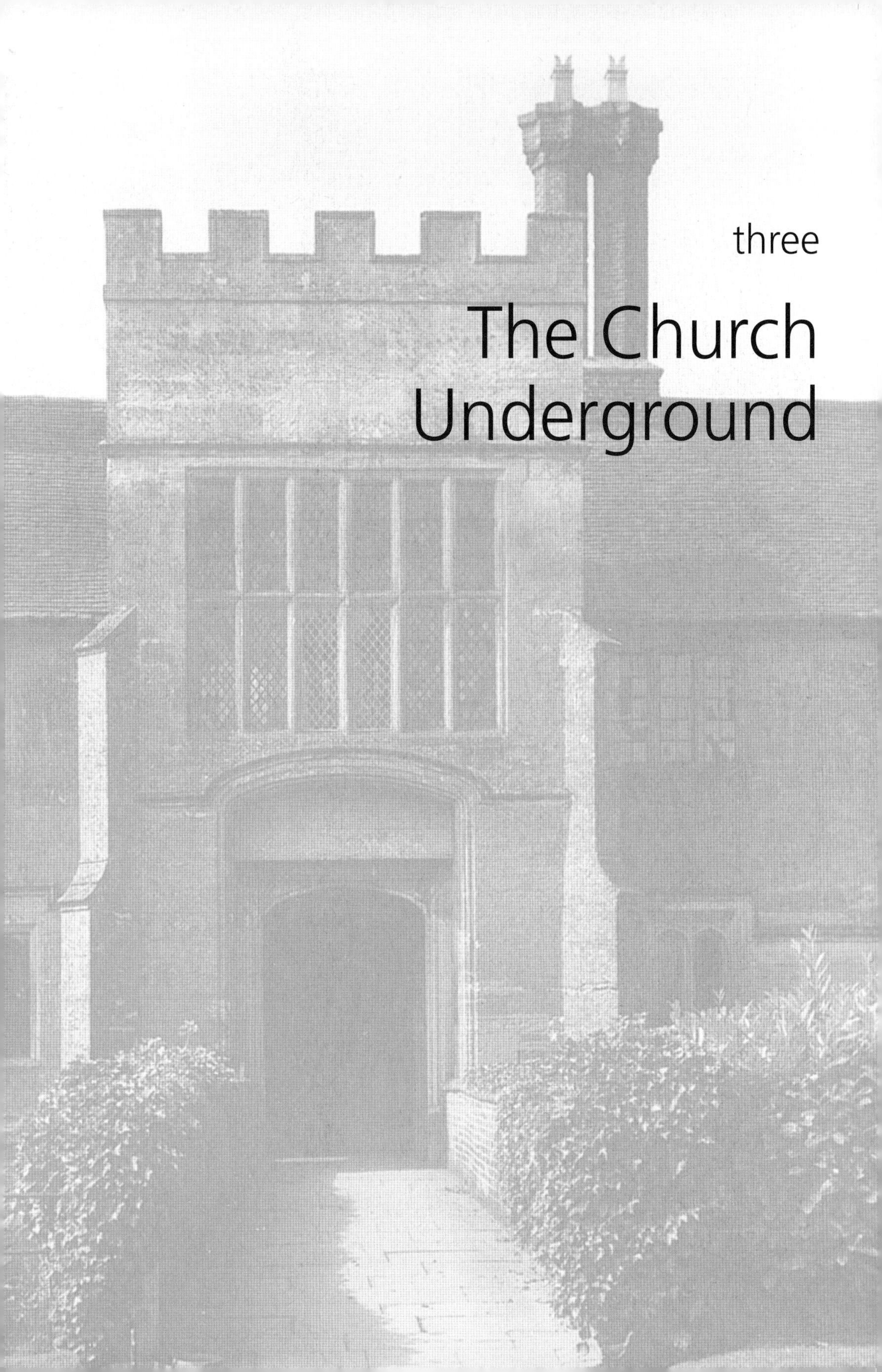

three

The Church Underground

Execution of Carthusian monks. After 1559 those who refused to attend Anglican church services (recusants) were fined and in the worst period of persecution, roughly between the Spanish Armada and the Gunpowder Plot, Catholicism was equated with treason and captured priests, mostly semi-nomadic Jesuits trained abroad, were hung, drawn and quartered. They were hunted down by poursuivants ('searchers') and it was a serious offence even to be in possession of 'massing stuff' – vestments, missals, pyxes, etc.

English priests were ordained abroad and smuggled back into England. Many of them were martyred after show trials before much feared judges such as Sir William Scroggs who cowed juries. 'You had better be rid of one priest than three felons', he thundered at the trial of Andrew Bromwich in 1679. Midland martyrs are commemorated in the names of modern Catholic schools, such as St Edmund Campion Secondary in Erdington, St John Wall and St Ambrose Barlow. Those pictured here are St Ambrose Barlow (left) and St Edmund Campion (right).

Middleton Hall 1892. In 1586 it was decided to adopt the strategy of hiding priests in the homes of Catholic gentry or yeomen farmers to serve an area. Conforming gentry were often tolerant of their recusant neighbours as they were interconnected by kinship or friendship. Secret chapels and hiding places were constructed in houses such as this to hide the priests and the massing stuff from the searchers.

A secret room in the roof of Middleton Hall, 1892.

Maps by John Speed of parts of Worcestershire (above) and Warwickshire (opposite) from 1602, marked to show houses of local Catholic gentry where known hides were constructed after 1586 for concealing priests or, later, Royalists: 1. Baddesley Clinton, 2. Perry Hall,

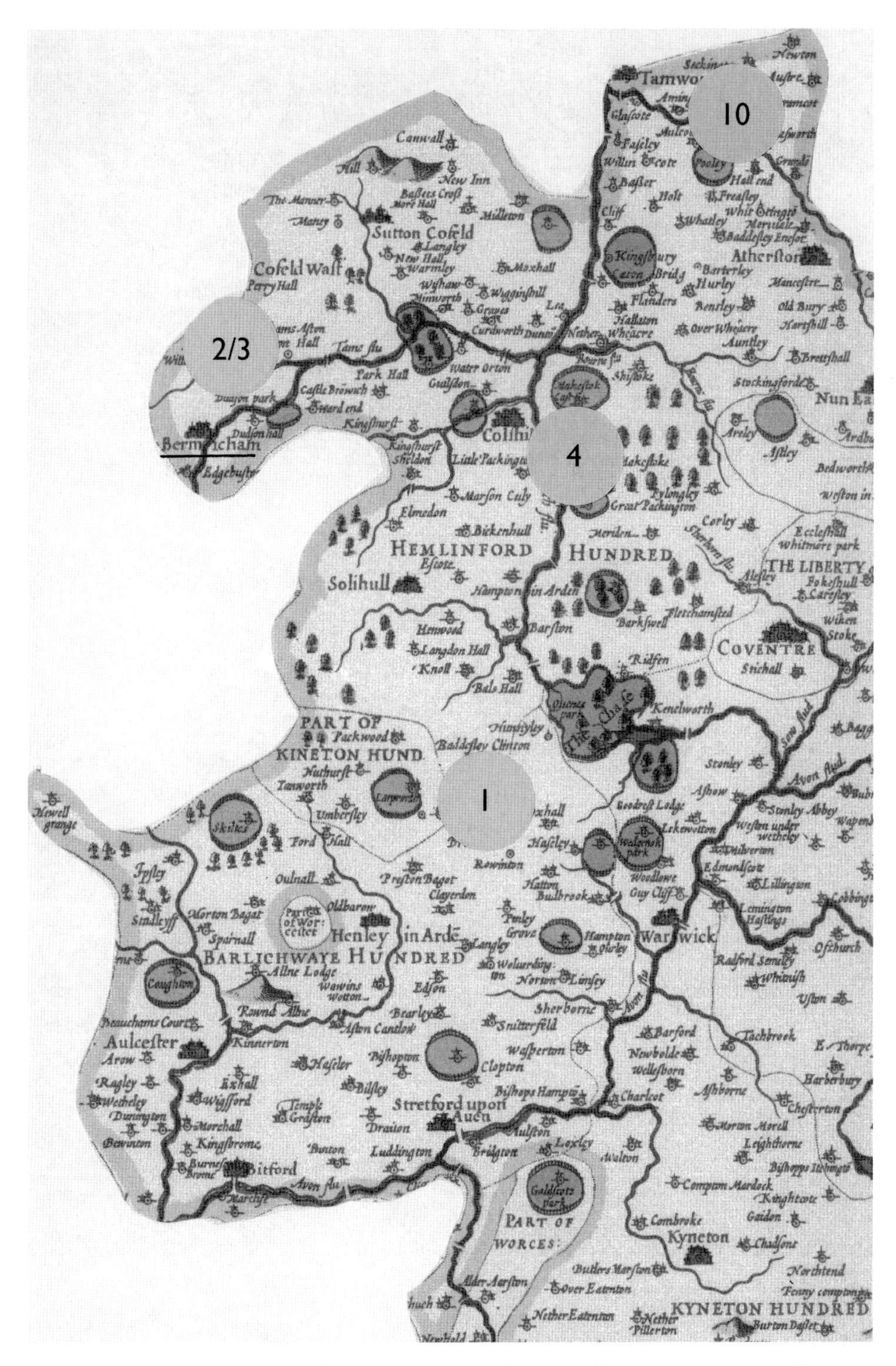

3. Aston Hall, 4. Packington Hall, 5. Harvington Hall, 6. Huddington Court, 7. Hindlip, 8. Moseley Old Hall, 9. Coughton Court, 10. Middleton Hall.

Baddesley Clinton, owned by the Ferrers family from 1509 to the twentieth century, has several priest holes, most famously one in the sewer in the west wing. The window above the waterline lit the cramped tunnel in which Gerard, Southwell, Garnet and four other priests hid for four hours in October 1591. Anne Vaux with a great show of indignation held off Topcliffe's searchers while the warm pallets were turned, vestments hidden and the priests secreted.

There is a lath and plaster hide in the roof to the south of the gatehouse shown here, at Baddesley Clinton. There is also a space behind the fireplace in the Moat Room entered through the floorboards of the solar or library above. Probably the work of the most expert hide-builder, Nicholas 'Little John' Owen, a Jesuit lay-brother and carpenter/mason whose ingenious work was carried out behind the disguise of Fr Garnet's servant 1588 until his death under torture in the Tower of London in 1606.

Huddington Court. Fr Nicholas Hart said Mass here for the Gunpowder Plotters in the early hours of 7 November 1605. There was a moving panel of lath and plaster hung on iron hinges and the chapel hide was entered by treading on a floorboard which released a latch in the panelling in the roof of the long block to the right.

Harvington Hall at Chaddesley Corbett contains eight hiding-places, the finest surviving series in the country. Rescued from disrepair in 1932, the house is owned by the Archdiocesan Historical Commission and is close to Hindlip House, near Worcester, the home of Humphrey's friend Thomas Habington. Harvington Hall had four hides around the great staircase almost certainly Owen's work, and a secret chapel decorated with the red and white drops of the Passion. Another in Dodd's Library is an example of the double bluff employed by Owen, a hide within a hide.

Opposite above: The secret chapel at Harvington Hall. The painted drops in red and white represent the blood and sweat of Our Lord at the Crucifixion.

Opposite below: Baddesley Clinton Hall library, 1896. This was reputedly the scene of the murder of a priest by one G. Brown.

Left: The hide in Dodd's Library, Harvington Hall. Having found the space behind the books, the priest-catchers would not have looked for an inner one.

Below: A recess in the corner of the banqueting hall at Harvington Hall conceals another hide, 1949.

The Moseley Old Hall hide used by Charles II on 9 September 1651. This Elizabethan house was owned by the Whitgreave family until 1925. In the attics there is a small hide in a gable which was probably for the massing stuff from the chapel close by.

A secret cupboard at Aston Hall marked by a hinged chain under the staircase in the passage leading from the Great Hall. The cupboard is probably from the Civil War period and the skeleton is for dramatic effect only!

Coughton Court was the home of the Throckmorton family from 1409 to 1946. The top floor of the gatehouse was used as the secret chapel and there is a 3-layered set of hides in the Tower Room. A Spanish leather altar, a rope ladder, a palliasse and a small piece of tapestry were found in the lowest level. Other smaller ones are said to exist.

A second chapel in the roof of Middleton Hall.

Left: The priest-hole at Boscobel House used by Charles II after the Battle of Worcester in September 1651.

Below: Packington Old Hall is of Elizabethan or Jacobean origin and Charles II spent a night here in 1651. There is a hide under the attic floorboards and behind the top left-hand light of the upper cruciform window to the right of the porch. (Information for this and above captions from *Secret Places* by Michael Hodgetts, Veritas 1989)

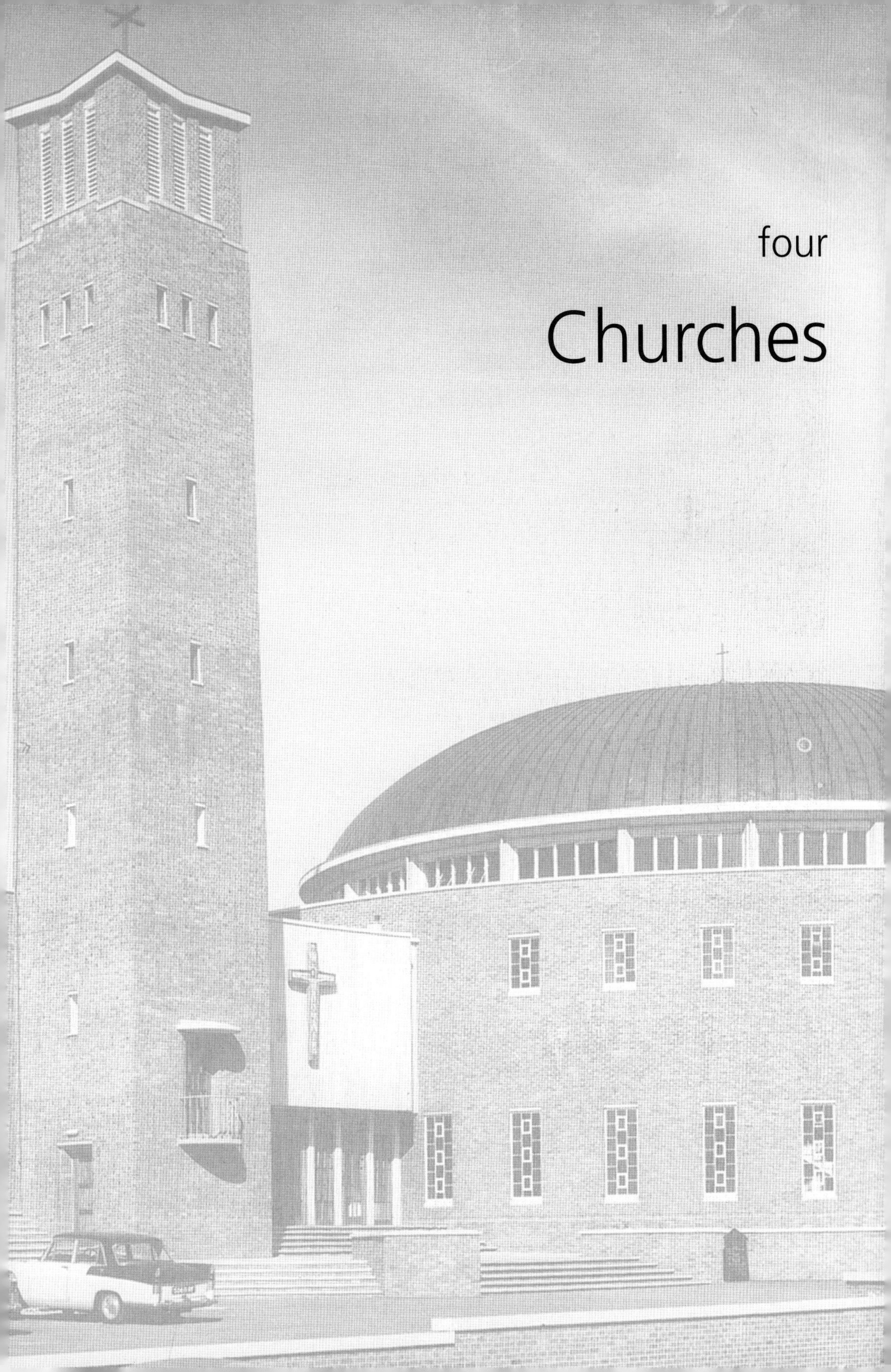

four

Churches

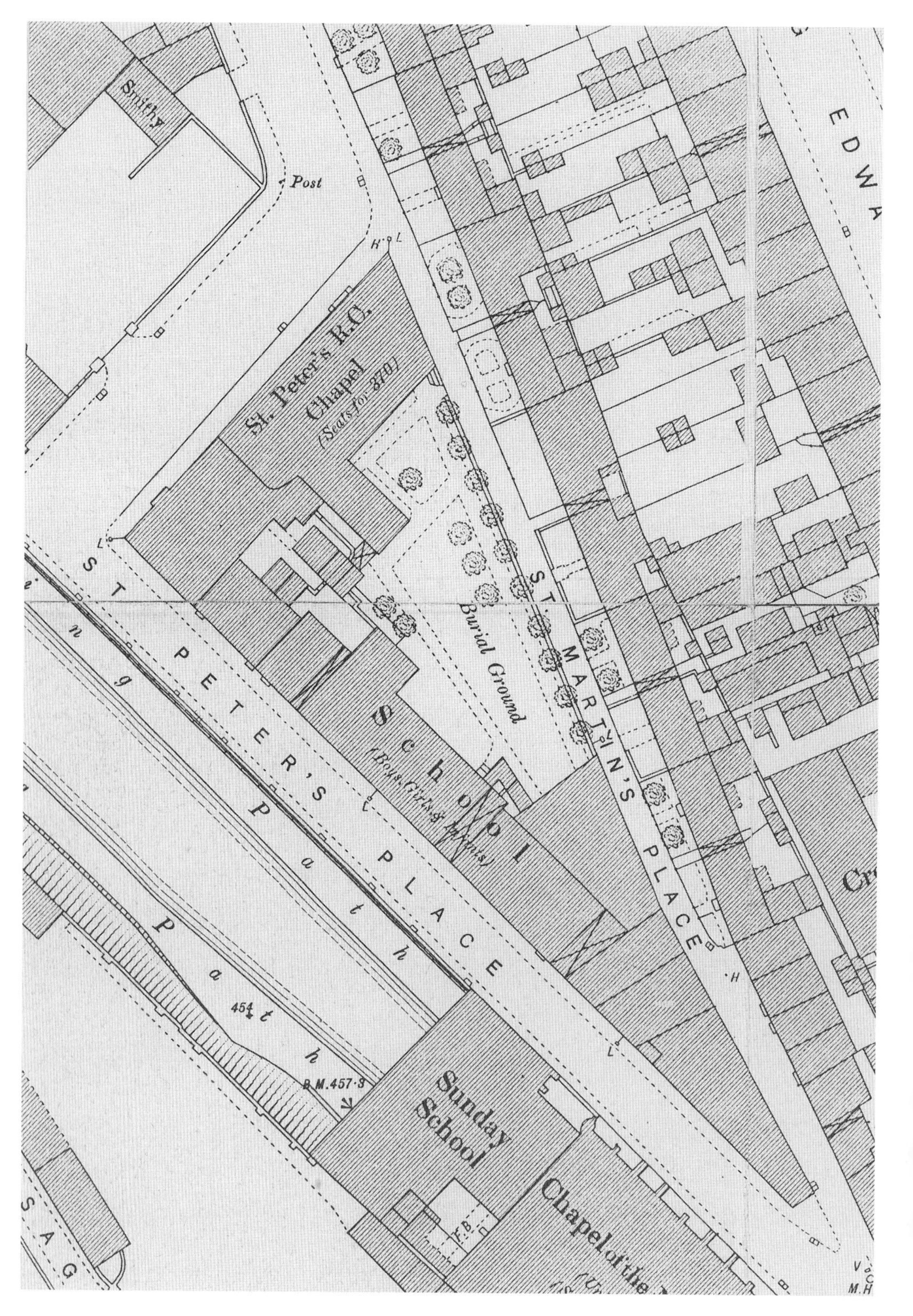
Smithy
Post
St. Peter's R.C. Chapel
(Seats for 370)
Burial Ground
ST. MARTIN'S PLACE
ST PETER'S PLACE
School
(Boys, Girls & Infants)
Path
Path
454
B.M. 457·3
Sunday School
Chapel of the
EDWA
SAG
F.B.

Deliberately unassuming in style, St Peter's was a redbrick structure with gothic windows, enlarged in 1871 and consecrated in 1933.

Right: Unusually, St Peter's had an inside gallery running along three sides and an apsidal chancel in which the altar was flanked by arched tribunes. It is seen here during demolition in 1967.

Opposite: This plan of St Peter's Place (*c.* 1800), shows the position of the Catholic chapel built in 1786, the only one to survive in Birmingham since the Reformation, with the school and burial ground also marked. St Peter's was demolished in 1967 during redevelopment of the city centre.

Above: The Franciscans eventually settled in Edgbaston after the destruction of their short-lived chapel in 1688, renting what became known as Mass House Farm from the Reeve family. In 1723 their school at Osmotherley was transferred there. Only after 1778 was the penalty of imprisonment abolished for Catholic priests and schoolmasters.

Left: St Anne's, Alcester Street, built 1884 on the site of a former gin distillery, Cardinal John Henry Newman opened the first proper Birmingham Oratory next to the site in 1849 in a house called 'Cardinal Newman's House' which became a school run by nuns after the Oratory moved to the Hagley Road, Edgbaston. St Anne's is now the home of the Oblates of Mary Immaculate.

Above: St Thomas and St Edmund of Canterbury was the church built by Fr Haig in 1848 after the original small chapel in Bell Lane was outgrown. The chapel was later reassembled in the grounds and became part of the school. In 1876 a small party of Benedictine monks arrived from Germany and built an abbey alongside, extending it in 1896-8. There were forty professed monks there in 1912. Their abbot was sent as chaplain to the nuns at Olton in a gentlemanly form of internment during hostilities, but they did a great deal of good work in Erdington until 1922, when the Order returned to Germany, with the Redemptorists taking their place. The building recently became an independent day school.

Right: Our Lady of Lourdes, Trittiford Road, Yardley Wood. The mission was established in 1931 and the church, a brick school hall, was opened in 1935. From 1951 priests from here also celebrated Mass at Glenavon Road, Warstock.

Right: Built on simple classical lines in 1802, St Michael's Moor Street was formerly the New Meeting Chapel, purchased by the Church in 1861. The St Nicholas' congregation, which had shared a building in Webb Lane with a school, moved here in 1862. At one time a centre for Italian expatriates, it acquired a Polish chaplaincy after the Second World War with a purpose-built Polish centre in Bordesley Street. Mass is said here in Polish and there is a beautiful mosaic Madonna inside.

Below: Jan (right) arrived in Britain after serving in the Polish Air Force during the Second World War and after incarceration in a Russian concentration camp. George (left), arrived a little later and went to Technical College in Birmingham, working here thereafter. Both have raised families here but have encouraged their children to keep in touch with their cultural roots by attending classes at the Polish Centre. Both feel their faith has been a strong influence in bonding the community in difficult times and remember when the present site of the centre was a school and graveyard for the church.

St Mary's, Vivian Road, Harborne was built in 1877. The first church had been opened by the Passionists in a former Weslyan chapel in 1870 which became a school in 1874. A Gothic revival building of red brick with stone dressings, it has a chancel, a nave of three bays, a south aisle and a south transept, with an octagonal bell-turret.

St Vincent de Paul, Vauxhall Grove. A school chapel in Ashted Row opened in 1884 but a new church opened here in 1930, serving also as a school hall. It forms the central feature of the school and is of red brick with a stone Venetian window at its west end.

Above: The laying of the foundation stone of a new church in Acocks Green by Bishop Ilsley, the Church of the Sacred Heart for the Deliverance of the Holy Souls, 1907. When the French nuns of Our Lady of Compassion arrived here in 1905, Mass was being said in a greenhouse, then a shed and then on the upper floor of their school. The church, built with the energy of Fr Gibbons, was known as the War Memorial Church as it daily commemorated those killed in action in both wars.

Opposite page
Above left: St Catherine of Siena, Bristol Street/Horse Fair. The original church was a gothic revival building of red brick with stone dressings opened in 1875. The nave of five bays was separated from wide aisles by red sandstone arcades and the rest of the interior was of yellow brick. The chancel, ambulatory and south chapel were added in 1893 and a tower with octagonal belfry and a squat stone spire date from 1909.

Above right: The church of the Sacred Heart and St Margaret Mary, Aston. An iron church dedicated to the Sacred Heart and St Thomas of Canterbury was opened in 1897 and then moved to Prestbury Road around 1915. The present church was opened in 1922 and consecrated in 1933. Italian Romanesque in style it is built of brindled brick with stone dressings, with a high five-storey northwest tower. The tympanum above the west door has a Crucifixion in mosaic. The interior is Byzantine with more mosaic figures in a small dome at the east end of the chancel.

Below: St Catherine of Siena, Horsefair. The new church has a distinctive circular shape and was built in the 1970s.

Left: St Patrick's, Spring Hill stands opposite the City Hospital on Dudley Road and its priest is Catholic chaplain there. It opened in 1895 after an iron church had replaced the former shed in 1876. Designed by Dempster and Heaton it is a redbrick building in Gothic style with a southwest octagonal bell turret.

Below: Mary the Mother of God, Shard End, 1983.

Above: A church garden-party of the 1950s reveals the less formal nature of a parish priest's relationship with his parishioners.

Below: Roman Catholic mortuary chapel at Witton cemetery. Dedicated to St Joseph and opened in 1850, this part of the church was designed by A.W. Pugin in the style of the fourteenth century. Extended in 1872, the nave of five bays is divided from a wide north aisle by a stone arcade with capitals of unusual design.

Birmingham Pilgrimage Sick and

Viron
elpers Lourdes 1959

St Mary's College, (Old Oscott) was renamed Maryvale by John Henry Newman. It was built in the 1790s where the imprisoned priest Andrew Bromwich had a house in the seventeenth century and it served as a boy's boarding school and seminary until the college moved to the new building at New Oscott in 1838. Newman returned here from Rome after his conversion and the Oratory was formally erected here in 1847. In 1851 it became an orphanage run by the Sisters of Mercy and the new church opened in 1937. It has been a teaching centre and Catholic Institute in recent years.

Above: New Oscott College was designed by Pugin and took St Mary's College students in 1838. Many famous Catholic clerics have served as Rectors or retired here and it was the location of John Henry Newman's famous 'Second Spring' sermon of 1852. Newman was here briefly himself under Cardinal Wiseman following his conversion and was confirmed in the chapel prior to his departure to Rome for his ordination as a Catholic priest. The college is still a seminary today. (Church history sourced for this chapter from the *Victoria History of the Counties of England, Vol. 7, Warwickshire*, Ed. W.B. Stephens, 1964)

Previous spread: Birmingham Pilgrimage to Lourdes, 1959. The photograph shows the sick and their helpers who came from right across the diocese.

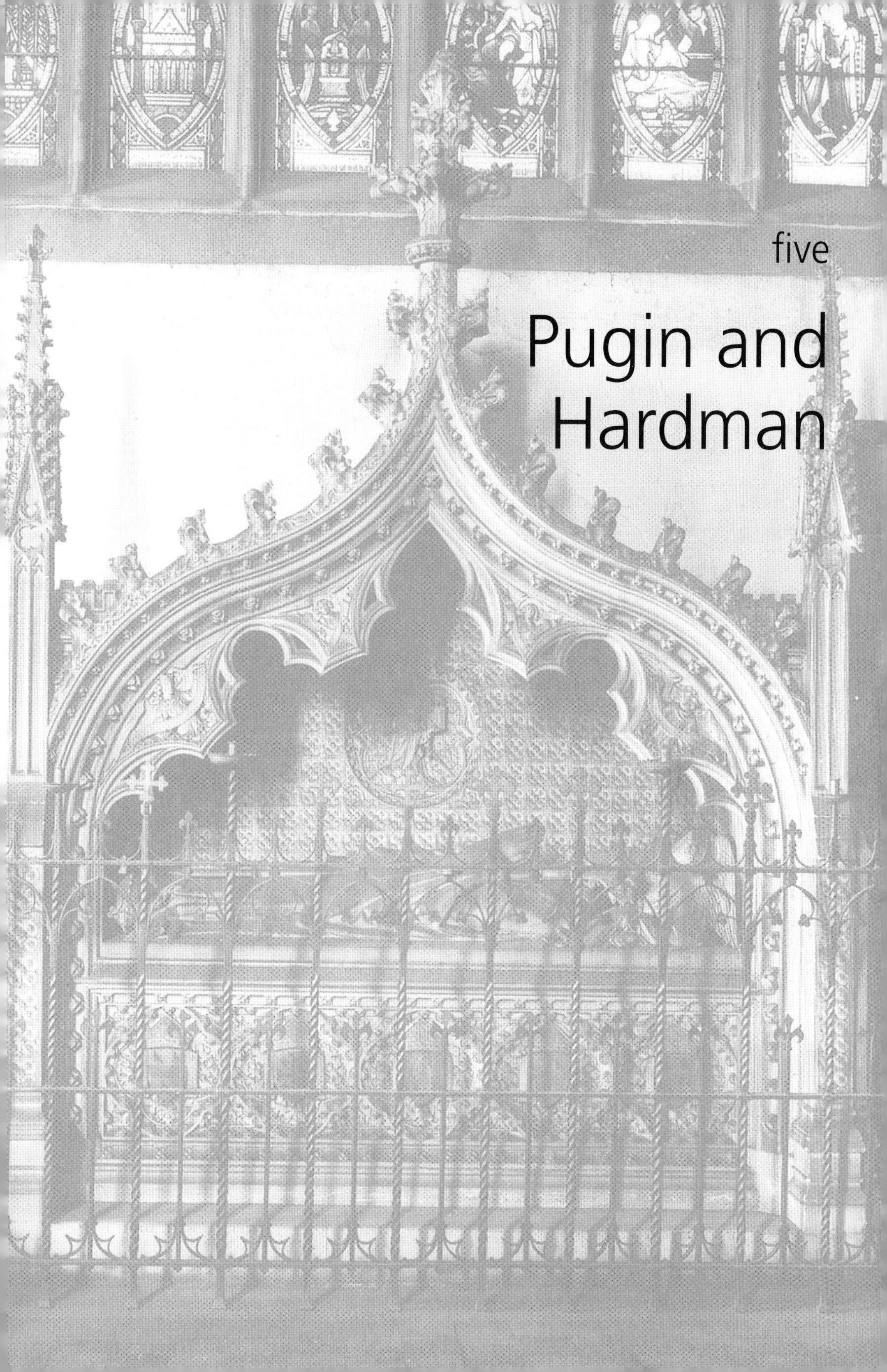

five

Pugin and Hardman

Above left: A.W. Pugin's book *Contrasts,* published in 1836, compared the Victorian Age unfavourably with the Middle Ages. Augustus Welby Pugin (1812-1852) converted to Catholicism in 1835 and under the patronage of the 16th Earl of Shrewsbury brought about a Gothic revival in English Catholicism, not just in architecture, but also in medieval craftsmanship in vestments, metalwork and stained glass. Birmingham and the Midlands gave him opportunities and an industrial power base to put his ideas into practice.

Above right: John Hardman junior (1811-1867) founded the firm of Hardman and Co. in 1838 to produce the large amount of metalware needed to decorate the churches Pugin was building. The Birmingham firm used the new industrial techniques of mass production to make Pugin's high quality designs affordable. Both he and his father, John Hardman senior, endowed the Cathedral richly and are buried in the crypt. The Hardman Company also made the face and hands of Big Ben at Westminster and did much of the interior work in the Houses of Parliament, also designed by Pugin.

Opposite above: These reliquaries containing chalices and pattens in pewter and gilt and a water jar were all designed by Pugin and made by the Hardman Company at various times from the mid-nineteenth century to the 1930s.

Opposite below: Tabernacle from Princethorpe Priory by P.P. Pugin showing a processional crucifix, candlesticks and ciboria all designed by A.W. Pugin. A telescopic crozier (left) belonging to Bishop Walsh was used when he was travelling and the other (right) was made for Bishop Glancey in 1924.

Above: Pugin and Hardman plate and monstrance made for Mgr John Roskell in 1932. St Chad's Cathedral candlesticks are from the Hardman collection and the sideboard from Leighton Hall. The monstrance is of gold, melted down from contributions by the congregation who wished to celebrate the Jubilee of a much-loved priest. It was made by H. Cooper.

Opposite: A green and gold cope made from ancient Florentine material in 1841 by 'Mistress Powell and daughters'. Lucy Powell, the wife of Hardman's partner William Powell, took the Misses Lucy and Winifred Brown into partnership for vestment making as the Gothic style gained popularity. An advertisement running from 1853 until the 1870s says they devoted themselves 'entirely to making Chasubles, Dalmatics, Copes, Albs, Surplices, etc…from the designs by the late A.W.N. Pugin Esquire' from their address at 13, Easy Row, Birmingham.

Above: The Ilsley vestments in St Chad's Cathedral which were presented to Archbishop Ilsley to mark his Golden Jubilee in the same year as his consecration as the first Archbishop of Birmingham in 1911. Glowing with gold even after nearly a century, they formed the centrepiece of a unique exhibition of the work of the Pugin and Hardman families held in the Cathedral crypt in May 2004, at which most of these photographs were taken.

Left: The Ilsley cope in gold and red depicting St Peter in white and blue. These vestments were made not by the Misses Brown but by nuns from convents all over the diocese. Lucy Powell died in 1863, Lucy Brown in 1897 and Winifred in 1900. All are buried in the crypt of St Chad's.

Ilsley chasuble, in gold and white with orphrey of the Crucifixion. Pugin had set the trend by borrowing copies of fourteenth-century originals from Dr Daniel Rock and reproducing them. He claimed to have replaced the 'filthy rags' Bishop Walsh inherited 'with silk and gold'. Bishop Baines complained to the Vatican but the new vestments were permitted after investigation.

Second Ilsley cope in gold and white bearing the Cathedral arms in red, gold and blue. The crozier bears an ivory Madonna and child. The sacred pallium was made of wool and was the personal gift of the Pope to a new Archbishop, having lain on the tomb of St Peter the night before despatch.

The monument to Bishop Walsh designed by Pugin in St Chad's Cathedral. Bishop Walsh consecrated the cathedral on 21 June 1841 and was buried in the clergy vault below St Peter's Chapel in the crypt on the Feast of St Chad, 2 March 1849. The effigy, carved by George Myers, shows the bishop in full pontificals with a roundel showing him holding a model of the cathedral, in the medieval manner. It was displayed at the Great Exhibition of 1851 a year before Pugin himself died.

A cope in yellow, ivory and green made for Archbishop Williams, *c.*1930. The seven Christian virtues are picked out in red around an overlay of the Annunciation. Archbishop Williams was deeply concerned with education and social issues and thirty new parishes were founded in his episcopate. He reformed the diocesan administration and instigated the restoration of Harvington Hall as a living monument to the English martyrs.

A close-up of Williams' cope showing the depiction of Christian virtues in Latin: from the left; wisdom, discernment, good counsel, courage, knowledge, faith and the fear of God.

PLEASE DO NOT
TOUCH
THANK YOU

Bookshelves designed by E.W. Pugin and containing medieval wood sculptures from the Netherlands. These were collected by Pugin and given to St Chad's where they are currently undergoing restoration.

Right: A nineteenth-century confessional.

Opposite: Monstrance, holy water-bucket and mitres designed by Pugin for St Chad's. The mitres are red velvet overlaid in ivory, jewelled and banded in the liturgical colours of yellow, green or red.

REQUIEM

Left: A brass lectern designed and made by Pugin and Hardman.

Right: Brass monuments were a staple of the Hardman Company's work. In the 1840s the cost of a brass varied between £7 and £100 depending on size and detail. Stained glass was also an artistic and decorative feature of many Midlands churches and Hardman was a major producer, advertising in every Catholic directory.

Opposite: The Hardman chantry in the crypt of the cathedral. John Hardman junior's portrait gazes at his own grave. Many of the Hardman family are buried here in this lavishly ornate and colourful expression of Pugin's ideas. The company still continues as John Hardman Studios in Lightwood Park working from original Pugin cartoons.

Left: The funeral pall of the 16th Earl of Shrewsbury, Pugin's patron, 1852. It was made by the Misses Brown at 3 Great Charles Street and commissioned by Edward Pugin, A.W. Pugin having died earlier the same year. The family motto 'Pres d'accomplir' is a little modest in John Talbot's case – he accomplished a very great deal.

Below: John Hardman junior gave to the Sisters of Mercy the convent of St Mary at Hunters Hill and his daughter Juliana was the first Superior in 1840. The present building is a reconstruction after the original was badly damaged by bombs in the Second World War.

six

Schools

Holy Souls Convent School, Acocks Green, *c.* 1926. There were two schools: one boarding and the other a day-school. Both were run by the Sisters of Our Lady of Compassion who arrived at Wilton House in 1905 and started the first school with a chapel on the first floor. Archbishop Ilsley died in 1926 and almost all of the 123 elementary schools existing in the diocese had been opened during his religious lifetime.

The Sisters with a little girl at her First Communion.

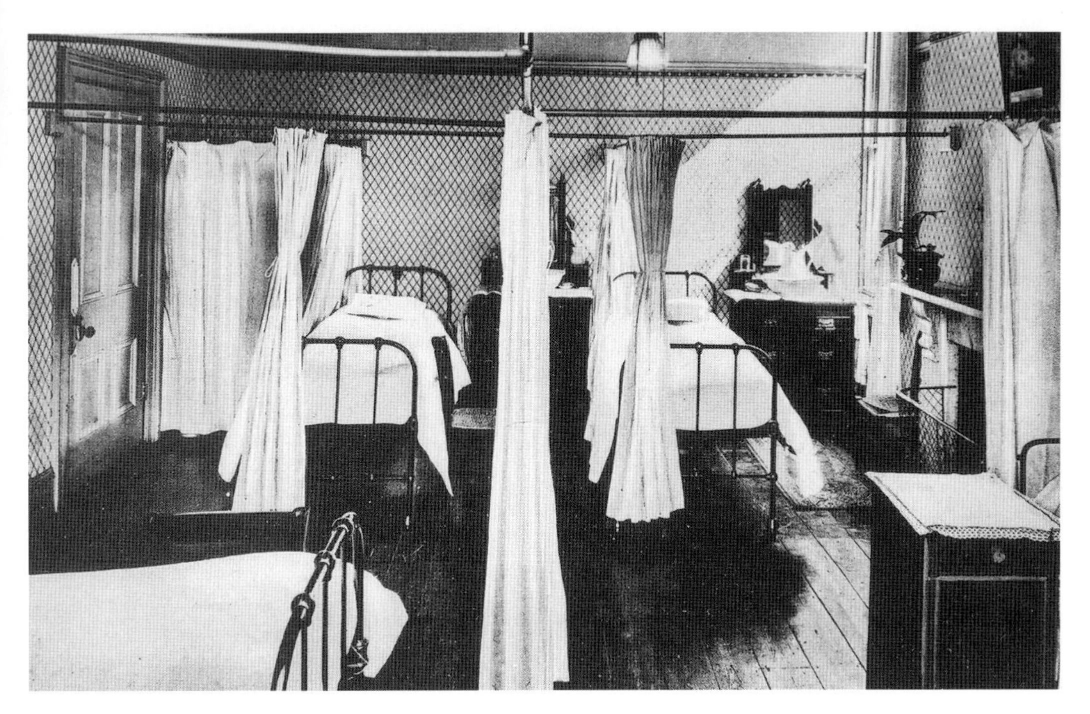

A dormitory at the boarding school, *c.* 1930. Conditions were quite Spartan – note the bare floorboards and the iron bedsteads.

A charming touch in the grounds – the Flowers Path. *Acocks Green was a quiet little village then where children could walk to school unattended and play unsupervised* - local resident of the time.

A pageant in the grounds on an international theme for the older girls, but they are still wearing their regulation black stockings!

Playing hockey in 1914 at St Paul's High School for Catholic Girls, Vernon Road, Edgbaston. The school was opened on 7 October 1908 by Lord Edmund Talbot and Bishop Ilsley, and was built and run by the Sisters of Charity of St Paul. The original school had three departments: Kindergarten, Secondary School and Pupil Teachers' Department.

The science laboratory in 1910. Girls were not usually taught science at that time. Most of the original pupils were fee-paying although there was later some small provision for poor girls. In the 1940s the school's status was changed to Voluntary Aided Grammar School and in 1975 it became a comprehensive. It is now called St Paul's School for Girls.

Dancing and drama in the Assembly Hall, *c.* 1951.

Science teaching has moved on - the teacher at St Paul's Girls School is now a woman, 1951. This room was later turned into the library.

A trigonometry lesson out of doors, 1951. The Sisters still wore the full habit at this time. It was later modified to a briefer coif, then a shorter blue habit and is no longer compulsory at all, although some prefer to retain a blue and white head-dress.

The library of St Paul's Girls School in the 1950s.

An art class at St Paul's Girls School in the 1950s.

A drill class in the Assembly Hall, 1914. Notice the gas lighting.

The geography room in the 1950s at St Paul's Girls School. The girls have been making Punch and Judy puppets and are showing them off with obvious enjoyment. Note the projection equipment at the back.

Right: Christine O'Grady and a classmate at a first Communion in St Joseph's Junior School.

Below: School prefects at Archbishop Ilsley Sixth Form College, 1961. Front row, left to right: Sandra Chance, Maureen Farmer, Elizabeth Porter, Vera McGuire, T. Bennett, Mary H., Sheila McAvee, Josephine Hughes, Antoinette Azzopard. Back row: Michael Duncan, Robert McMonagle, Ian Murdoch, Donald Hayes, Kyran Brennan, John Neild, Paul Byrne, Bernard Wall, Max Auli, David Byrne, Peter Demsford.

The school chapel St Paul's Grammar School, Vernon Road, Edgbaston, *c.* 1950. The statues are of St Paul and Our Lady. The chapel was also used by the attached convent, a daughter house of the Sisters of Charity of St Paul, who ran the school. Their emblem is on the chancel arch.

Above: A sixth-form class at Archbishop Ilsley Sixth Form College with the head teacher Mr Bishop, *c.* 1960. Archbishop Ilsley was founded in 1910 when Edward Ilsley was very concerned for the provision of Catholic secondary schools in the diocese so that the groundwork laid in the elementary schools would be built upon and young people not lost to the faith.

Right: St Anne's R.C. School, Alcester Street, 1933. The school occupied the building formerly called Cardinal Newman's House, the first home of the Birmingham Oratory in 1849. After the Oratorians moved to the Hagley Road in 1852, the school was run by the nuns at St Anne's, now Oblates of the Immaculate Conception.

Above: Girls from St Paul's Grammar School visiting St Peter's Square, Rome with their teachers, Sisters of the Charity of St Paul. St Peter's in Rome is formally the Basilica of St Peter and St Paul and so a visit there would have special significance for the girls. Note that everyone entering St Peter's has their heads and arms covered (women) or are in long trousers (men). This dress code is still in force in 2004 to the extent that tourists have to cover bare shoulders (women) and legs (men). The statue on the left is of St Paul.

Above: Frances Andrews, Bernadette Madden and Wendy Smith representing Birmingham Schools at a gymnastic performance for the Physical Education Association of Great Britain and Northern Ireland in Derbyshire, *c.* 1970.

Right: Senior students from Archbishop Ilsley School face the future with happiness and confidence in this delightful photograph from 1961. The students are Bernard Wall, Peter Demsford, Donald Hayes, Max Auli and John Nield.

Opposite below: A visit to the Houses of Parliament by a group of St Paul's girls and a meeting with the Edgbaston MP, Sir Peter Bennett, *c.* 1960.

St Chad's School trip to the Skerries, Dublin in 1954. The boys' school was in Shadwell Street and the Girls' in Brierley Street. The headmistress seen here is Sister Etha and Miss McCarthy is on the back row, left.

The gymnasium at St Paul's Girls' School, *c.*1960.

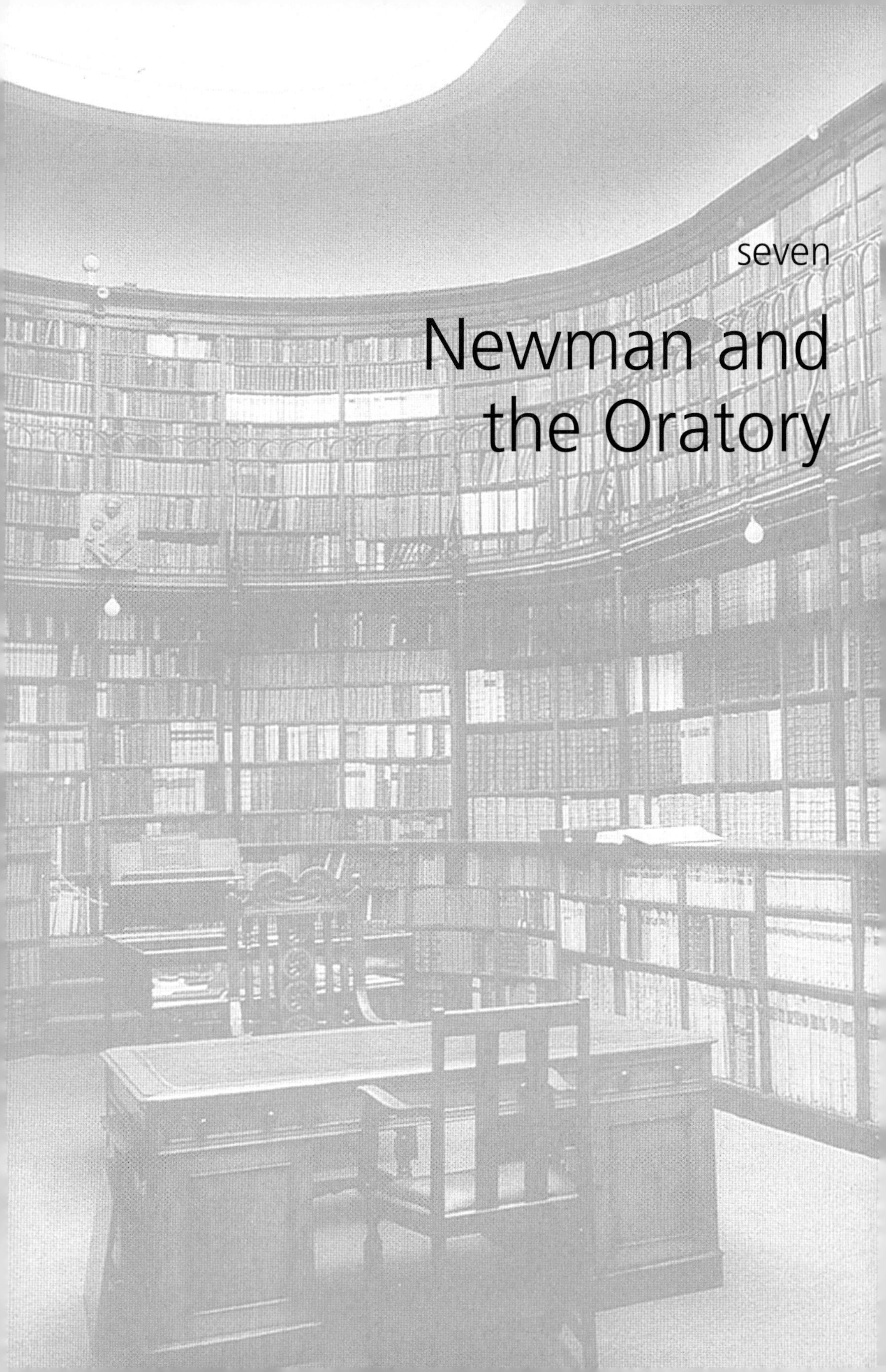

seven

Newman and the Oratory

England in 1850 was in a fever of religious and political frenzy. Catholicism had a new high profile in the wake of the converts from the Oxford Movement and the church hierarchy was about to be restored. *Punch* expressed this in satirical cartoons such as this one which caricatures John Henry Newman on the far right.

The English Oratory was formally 'erected' at Maryvale on the 1 February 1848 but the doors really opened at Alcester Street, Birmingham on 26 January 1849 in what became known later as 'Cardinal Newman's House', and small chapel. When the Oratorians moved to the Hagley Road, the house in Alcester Street was turned into a school run by the Sisters of Mercy and a church built beside it, St Anne's, in 1884.

The Oratory, Hagley Road, *c.* 1902. In 1852 John Henry Newman had moved the Oratorians here and a small group under Fr Frederick Faber had gone to London to found an Oratory there.

Left: A view of the Old Church and old High Altar on St Philip's Day, *c.* 1853. St Philip Neri was the patron saint of the Order. The building was a simple one with a roof from an abandoned factory. In 1858 an aisle was added by John Hungerford Pollen and then an apse and two transepts.

Below: The interior of the new church built by Doran Webb as a memorial to Cardinal Newman after his death in 1890. It was opened in 1911 and the total length is 198 feet with a total width of 57 feet. The marble columns in the nave came from Serravezza and were shipped in pairs on a little steamer that made six voyages. They arrived in Birmingham on canal barges.

Baptistry and aisle at the Oratory, 1911.

Altar of the Sacred Heart and chapel of St Charles Borromeo, Birmingham Oratory, *c.* 1920.

Above: Cardinal Newman's room, left untouched since his death. Behind the camera was originally his bed, but this area was converted into a private chapel when he became a cardinal and he then had a separate bedroom.

Opposite above: The library at the Oratory. Elgar's original score of the *Dream of Gerontius* used to lie on the desk here but it is now archived more securely! Newman wrote the text of this and published it in 1865. His famous hymn 'Lead, kindly light' had been written in 1833 and a handwritten copy dated 1865 was recently found bound into a biography of Newman at Birmingham Central Library. It is possibly in Newman's own hand and signed by him.

Right: Oratorians dressed all in black with a small white collar which *Punch* caricatured to give them a grim aspect.

Below: Society subjected to 'Puseyite' (Catholic/Anglo-Catholic) pressure in another *Punch* cartoon, 1850. Newman is probably represented by the figure on the bottom far left.

Oratorian. "Is your Mistrass within, my dear?"
Maid-of-All-Work. "Oh, help! halp! here's a Bogie, Missus! help! help!"

A PAGE FOR THE PUSEYITES.

Lady Georgina Chatterton was typical of Newman's correspondents who were attracted to the Catholic Church but hesitated about converting fearing social ostracism. In 1863 she wrote to him, 'From the impression your writings have made upon me I…think you would be glad to assist with advice a person who is passing through the doubts which you have encountered.' In 1865 she was received into the Church and continued to correspond with Newman over minor difficulties.

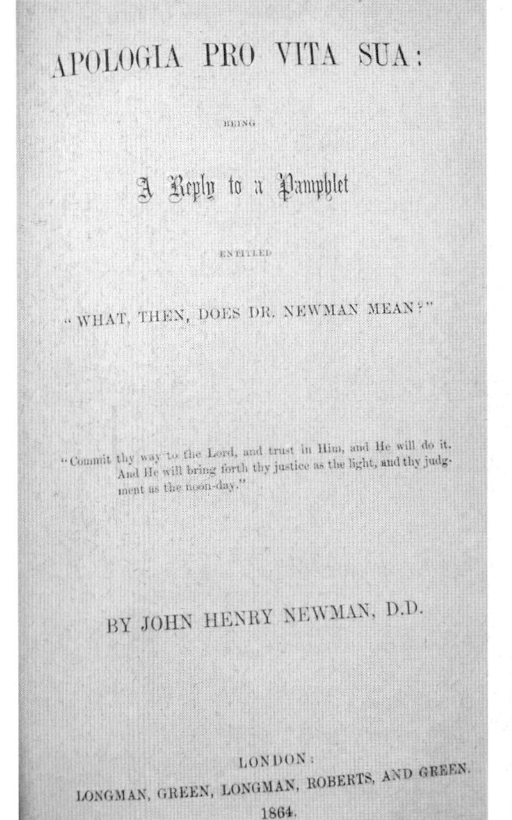

APOLOGIA PRO VITA SUA:

BEING

A Reply to a Pamphlet

ENTITLED

"WHAT, THEN, DOES DR. NEWMAN MEAN?"

"Commit thy way to the Lord, and trust in Him, and He will do it. And He will bring forth thy justice as the light, and thy judgment as the noon-day."

BY JOHN HENRY NEWMAN, D.D.

LONDON:
LONGMAN, GREEN, LONGMAN, ROBERTS, AND GREEN.
1864.

A first edition, held in Birmingham Central Library, of Cardinal Newman's spiritual autobiography *Apologia Pro Vita Sua,* written in 1864 in reply to a stinging attack on his integrity by Charles Kingsley. The book had a major influence after it first appeared serialised in *The Month*.

John Henry Newman, *c.* 1865.

Left: Fr Paul Chavasse, Superior of the Birmingham Oratory, during the blessing of the palms at the start of High Mass at the Oratory, Palm Sunday, 2004. (*Birmingham Catholic News*)

Below: The Oratory ran an orphanage for boys in Oliver Road managed by Fr Austin Mills who spent nearly every afternoon there and was much loved by the boys. St Philip's Orphanage moved to new quarters at Chad Valley House in 1934 and the move is recorded in this photograph. Not all the furnishings went in the van - some rolls of linoleum travelling on a handcart borrowed from the Scouts went literally downhill!

A statue of John Henry Newman at the Brompton Oratory in London which was established under the leadership of Fr Faber in 1849. Cardinal Newman's letters and diaries show frequent tensions between them, but the Oratory in London flourished.

Ambrose St John was Cardinal Newman's closest friend and was headmaster of the Oratory School until his death in 1875. The cardinal was heartbroken at his death and left instructions that when he himself died he was to be buried in the same grave.

Playground of the old Oratory School in 1891. The school was a boarding school for the sons of gentlemen and has been attended by some famous men: J.R.R. Tolkien, Hilaire Belloc, G.K. Chesterton, future Dukes of Norfolk and the holder of a Victoria Cross in the First World War - and several fine Newman scholars.

John Henry Newman was created a cardinal in 1885. This portrait was taken in Birmingham when the cardinal was very old – he remained mentally alert to the last.

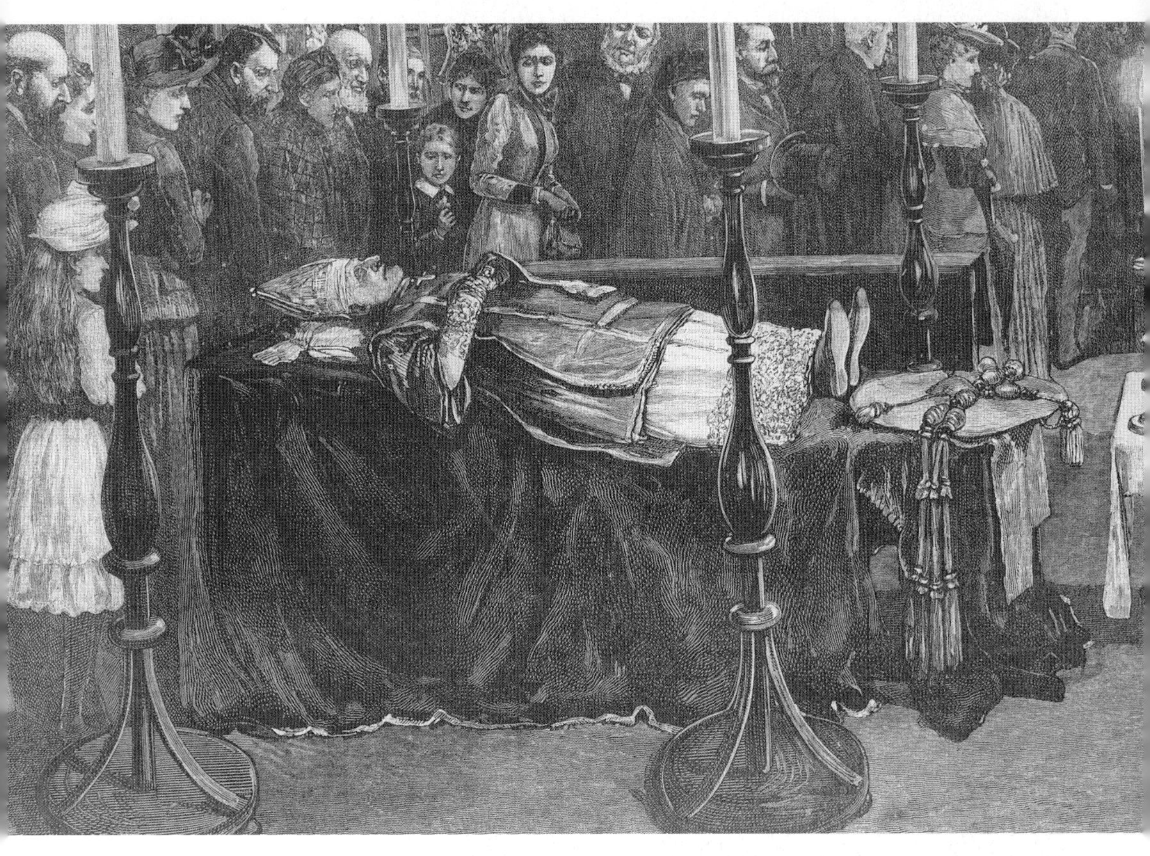

Cardinal Newman died in August 1890 at the Oratory. This drawing of his lying-in-state was published in the *Illustrated London News*. It was claimed in all his obituaries that England had lost a great man.

Above: Cardinal Newman was buried at Rednal in the Oratorian cemetery, in the same grave as Ambrose St John as he had wished. His coffin bore his motto, 'Cor ad cor loquitur' (Heart speaks unto heart), taken from St Francis de Sales, and his epitaph, inscibed on his memorial stone in the cloister of the Oratory, is 'Ex umbris et imaginibus in veritatem', (From shadows into truth). By coincidence, the yellow St John's Wort bushes planted in memory of Ambrose St John were in full flower.

PRAYER

TO OBTAIN THE BEATIFICATION OF

John Henry Cardinal Newman

O LORD JESUS CHRIST, Who, by the working of miracles, hast deigned to honour Thy loving servants, we beseech Thee to glorify, through the intercession of Thy Immaculate Mother, Thy servant John Henry Newman by evident signs and wonders, so that, for the exaltation of Thy name and the salvation of souls, he may, by Thy power, be declared blessed. *Amen.*

(Indulgence of 200 days)

"*As I came from Thee, as I am made through Thee, as I live in Thee, so, O my God, may I at last return to Thee, and be with Thee for ever and ever.*"

NEWMAN: Meditations and Devotions.

IMPRIMATUR

✠ JOSEPH

Archiepiscopus Birmingamiensis

November 12th, 1952

Left: Cardinal Newman was pronounced the Venerable John Henry Cardinal Newman by Pope John Paul II in 1991. The cause for his beatification proceeds.

eight

Convents

Mother Cecilia Auterson, Superior General of the Sisters of Charity of St Paul, 1953-68. The order was founded by Mother Genevieve Dupuis, a nun from Chartres, when she came to Banbury with Sister Joseph Marie Sapiens at the invitation of Fr William Tandy in June 1847. Their task was to provide elementary education for the Catholic poor. Strongly supported by Bishop Ullathorne, the Sisters opened a school in Birmingham in 1853 and later an orphanage.

St Paul's Convent, Selly Park, was founded 1864 when the mother house of the order moved here from Banbury. A new chapel was built in 1915. Active in teaching and nursing, the Sisters were asked by Bishop Ullathorne to take on his first Poor Law school for abandoned children, St Paul's at Coleshill. After the foundation of the Diocesan Rescue Society, they were to play a vital part in the running of Fr Hudson's Homes.

Dowell's Retreat, Warner Street, 1932.

Ravenhurst Manor House was acquired by the Sisters of St Anne's Convent of Mercy and they occupied it in 1860. Other buildings were added and it remained as a convent until it was bombed in the Second World War.

Above: St Anne's Convent, Camp Hill, 1933. The Sisters of Mercy were very active in Birmingham.

Left: Mother Cecila Auterson, Superior General, with Pope Paul VI and Mother Maria Pia Sheehan in Rome, *c.* 1960.

The Noviciate, Selly Park, *c.* 1910.

St Genevieve's Cloister, Selly Park, *c.* 1920

These young nuns are seen at their clothing ceremony (First Profession) in 1966. Having entered in wedding dresses and attended by the bridesmaids behind them, they left the service to reappear clothed as nuns.

Final Profession at St Paul's Convent, Selly Park, 1988. Habits have been modernised and they now do not have to wear religious dress at all unless they wish. In this happy photograph they are seen with Archbishop Maurice Couve de Murville. All Sisters wear the medal of the Order and sometimes also the distinctive head-dress on more formal occasions.

Belgian refugees at Moor Green House, 1914.

Previous page: Cardinal Godfrey, Cardinal Protector of the Order in the chapel, Selly Park. This beautiful chapel is the spiritual powerhouse of the convent with an atmosphere of calm and tranquillity. There is some fine stained glass depicting the arrival of Mother Dupuis and Saint Genevieve. There is now a gallery complete with CCTV and an induction loop so that elderly and infirm sisters in wheelchairs from the infirmary can attend services.

Above: Sister Marie Francis at Woodville mother and baby home in Raddlebarn Road, Selly Oak, *c.* 1950. This building is now St Mary's Hospice.

Right: Maryvale, formerly Oscott College, was run as an orphanage by the Sisters of Mercy 1851-1980.

Left: Sacred Heart Chapel, Maryvale, the oldest public chapel to the Sacred Heart in Great Britain. Maryvale is now an institute with an educational function.

Below: Sister Ursula Halpin in the playroom, Besford Court School for children with learning difficulties, formally one of Fr Hudson's Homes.

Opposite above: The Sisters of Charity of St Paul were heavily involved in nursing as well as teaching and staffed St Gerard's Hospital at Coleshill, part of Father Hudson's Homes. Their patients were often children from the Birmingham slums where ill nourishment and tuberculosis and other serious illnesses were rife. This photograph shows the open-air ward which was thought at the time to benefit TB patients.

Opposite below Another view of the open-air ward, *c.* 1920.

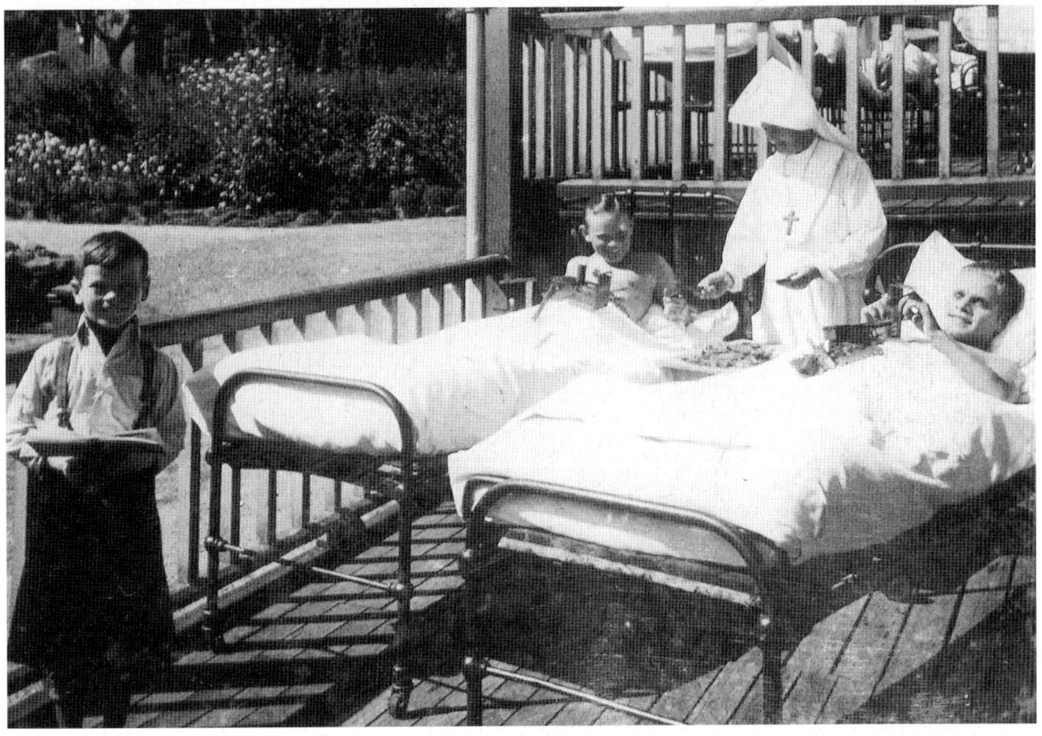

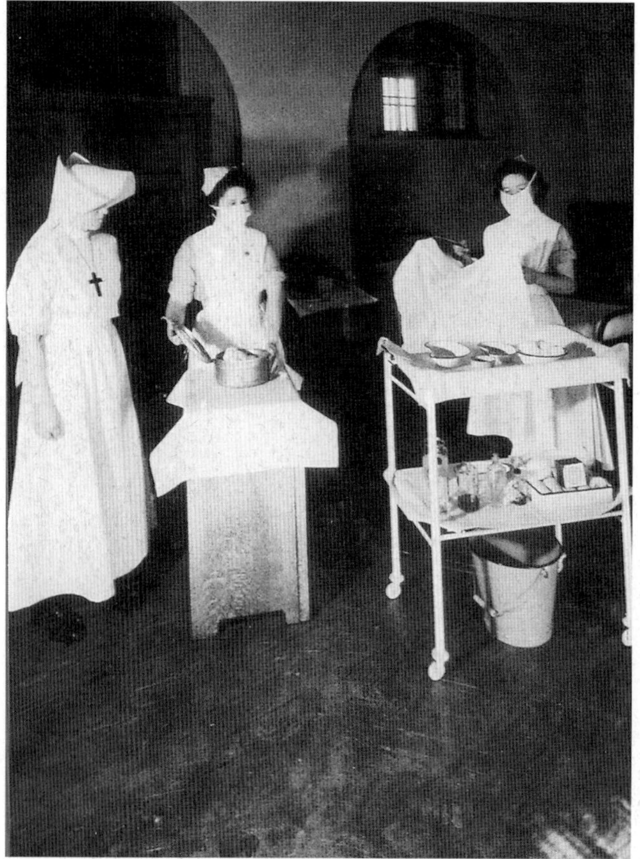

Above: The Sisters ran a teaching hospital and worked alongside the student nurses. This photograph was taken outside the main entrance of the hospital in front of the statue of St Gerard.

Left: Preparing for an operation, *c.* 1930.

Opposite below: Anne Bright Weston House, 1994. Sister Maria Dempsey is seen here with some of the residents. Many of the Sisters of St Paul live in small communities devoting themselves to work such as this. Others live together in small groups and work in the community around them, teaching, visiting the sick and elderly or running a place such as Fireside, a hostel for the homeless.

The Saltley Book of the Dead was a huge volume crafted in medieval style by the Carmelite nuns of Yardley for the Very Revd John Power, parish priest of the Rosary Church, Saltley. It records the anniversaries of people who have died and is full of bright colour and gold leaf. Despite its ancient appearance, it was created in 1934. The convent no longer exists but the volume is kept in the Archdiocesan Archives at Cathedral House.

Above: Sister Francis of Assisi on her 100th birthday in the infirmary, Selly Park, 2001. Sick and elderly nuns are nursed in the well-staffed hospital wing and remain very much part of the community. Sister Francis had not just a card from the Queen (held left) but also a blessing from the Holy Father (on the right). Sprightly and fully alert, she was visited by Lord Mayor Teresa Stewart and died peacefully a few months later.

Right: Mother Geneviève Dupuis, founder of the Sisters of Charity of St Paul in England.

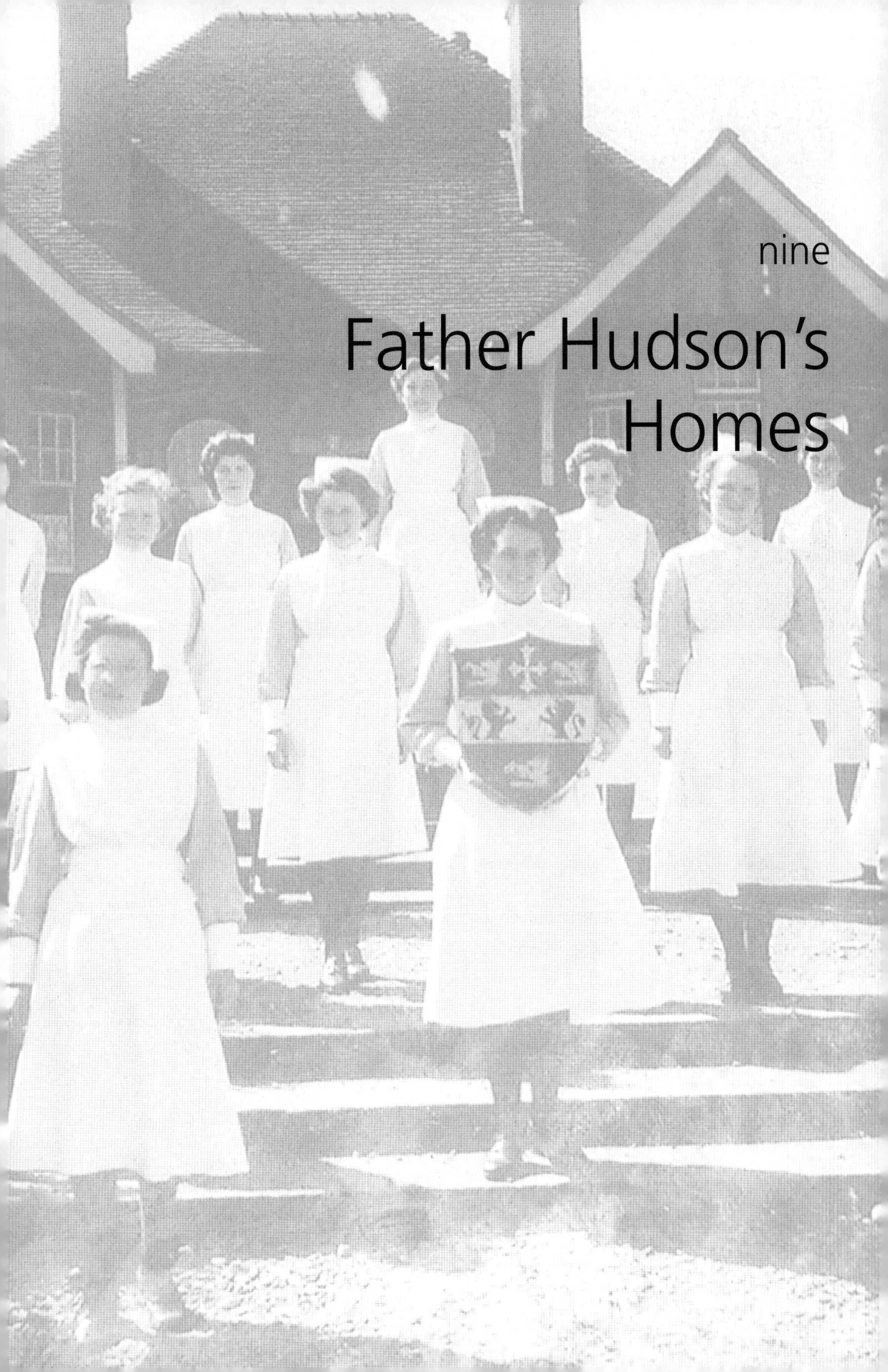

nine

Father Hudson's Homes

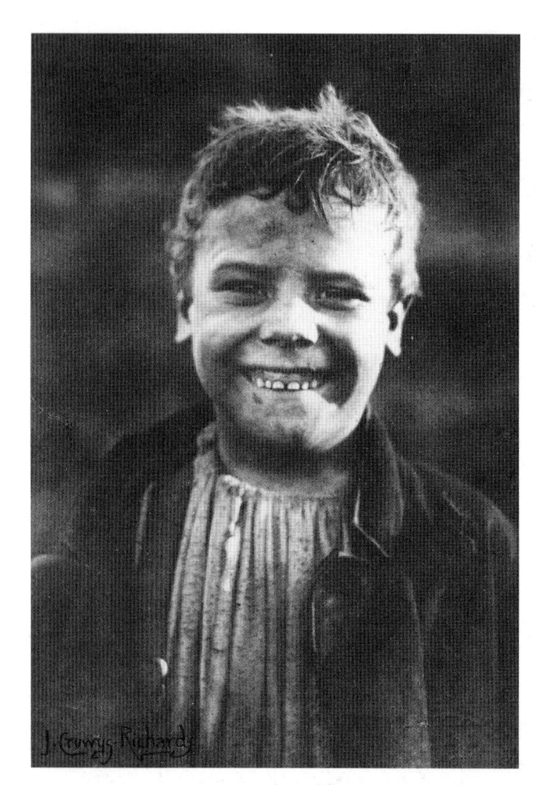

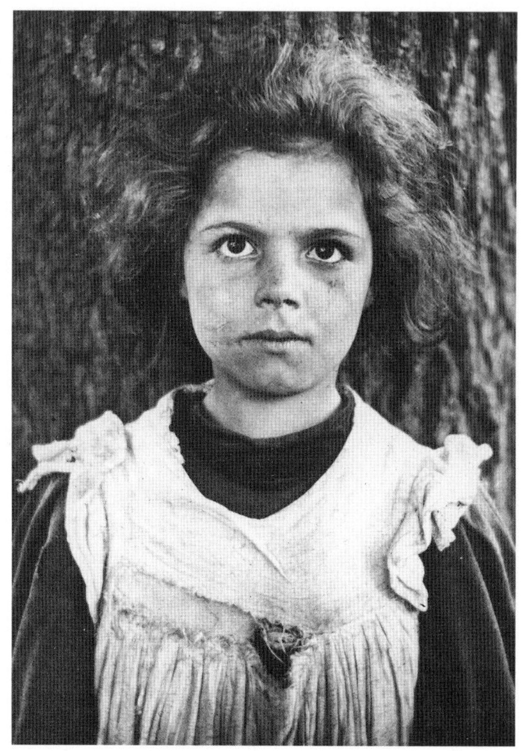

A boy and a girl from the backstreets of Birmingham having a day out in Sutton Park with the Cinderella Club, *c.* 1910. Many children lived in conditions of social deprivation and sometimes physical and moral danger. In 1989 Bishop Ilsley made it a diocesan priority to rescue and save the faith of Catholic homeless and destitute children.

Opposite: In 1902 the Birmingham Diocesan Rescue Society was founded and this front page of *The Fold*, its magazine, lists the homes it managed.

The Birmingham Diocesan Rescue Society,

For the Protection and Rescue of Homeless and Friendless Catholic Children.

President:
HIS LORDSHIP THE BISHOP OF BIRMINGHAM.

Honorary Secretary:
REV. GEORGE V. HUDSON, COLESHILL, BIRMINGHAM.

RESCUE COMMITTEE:

CHAIRMAN—HIS LORDSHIP THE BISHOP.

VICE-CHAIRMAN—THE VERY REV. CANON KEATING, D.D.

The Committee considers all cases of Destitute Catholic Children, and decides how they are best dealt with.

Homes and Institutions to which the Children can be sent:—

1. ST. EDWARD'S HOME FOR BOYS. For homeless boys. (The Building Fund at present amounts to £1,750.)
2. NAZARETH HOUSE, OXFORD. For homeless girls.
3. ST. PAUL'S HOME, COLESHILL. Certified School for boys.
4. ST. JOSEPH'S HOME, HANDSWORTH. Certified School for girls.
5. ST. MARY'S HOME, MARYVALE. Certified School for girls.
6. CATHOLIC WORKING BOYS' HOME, 102, MOSELEY ROAD, BIRMINGHAM. For boys over 14.
7. ST. ANTHONY'S HOME, BATH STREET, BIRMINGHAM. For girls over 14.
8. CATHOLIC BRANCH OF THE CRIPPLED CHILDREN'S UNION. For crippled children under 14.
9. CATHOLIC EMIGRATING ASSOCIATION. For the emigration of Catholic boys and girls.

The organ of the Society is "THE FOLD," published quarterly. 6d. a year, post free. Free to Subscribers. Apply, "The Editor," Coleshill, Birmingham.

No. 3 Court, Adams Street, Birmingham, *c.* 1900.

The Workhouse Union Buildings, Kings Norton, 1935. Before the advent of the Welfare State homeless children often ended up in places like these, although Dr Barnardo's and the NSPCC took in children in physical want or danger too.

Left: Fr George Vincent Hudson (1873-1936) was ordained in 1898 at Oscott College and appointed parish priest of Coleshill. When the Diocesan Rescue Society was set up, Fr Hudson became heavily involved in the foundation and management of many of the homes and over the course of time they became known locally as 'Father Hudson's Homes'. He was also instrumental in helping a large number of these youngsters to start new lives in Canada.

Below: St Edward's Home for Boys opened in 1906 with space for 120 boys. Like the other homes, it was run by the nuns of Selly Park, the Sisters of the Charity of St Paul. Mother Aloysia Fleming was Mother Superior here for the first ten years.

St Vincent's Home for Working Boys Cycling Club in the 1930s. The home was set up by Fr Hudson in 1901 to help with the aftercare of boys leaving St Paul's School and Home that had been set up before the Diocesan Rescue Society. After 1902 it was at 102 Moseley Road and accommodated forty-five Catholic boys whom it helped into work with Birmingham firms. The boys' earnings helped run it along with subscriptions and money from the Board of Guardians. It also provided leisure facilities and encouraged self-improvement.

St Edward's Junior School, opened on the Coleshill site in 1914 and could accommodate 160 children in four classrooms.

St Georges' and St James' Homes were founded in 1923 for boys from five to eleven years in smaller 'cottage homes'. They carried distinctive majolica medallions of a mother and child on the front.

Probably the Babies' Home, Coleshill, or, as it was called in 1910, Our Lady's Home for Babes. St Anthony's in Howard's Road, Handsworth, had probably originally taken in what were then called 'fallen girls' but had became too small. Efforts were made to place the young mothers in domestic service rather than allowing them to keep charge of their babies.

Setting off for the annual camp, *c*.1930.

St Gerard's Hospital, originally built as an infirmary for children, opened in 1913 and was run by the Sisters. It took eighty-three patients in the first eight months, thirty-eight of which had tuberculosis which was treated in open-air wards. The hospital went on to train nurses for the nursing of sick children and also, after 1931, in Domestic and Commercial Science at its St Philomena's School.

A picnic in the grounds for sick children, some of whom appear to have arrived at the hospital very malnourished.

Story-time outside, *c.* 1920. The fresh air of Coleshill was a welcome change for the children from Birmingham's slums.

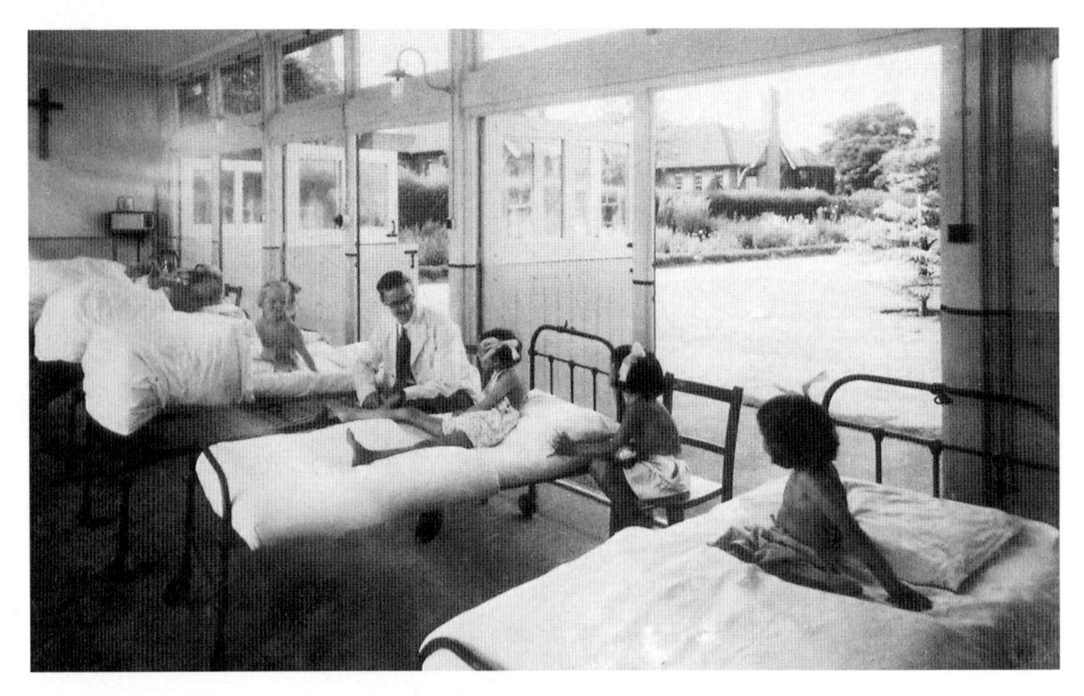

A children's ward, *c.* 1920. The children had the best of medical care and St Gerard's Orthopaedic Hospital had the services of Birmingham consultants as well as their own staff. Non-Catholic children from the Poor Board were taken as well as the Catholic children from the homes.

Above: Nurses posing for a photograph, having completed their training, display their new hospital badges. Nurses had their own hostel in the grounds.

Right: Besford Court Home was for what we would now call children with learning difficulties. The children were treated with the most up-to-date methods as the annual reports show and farm work and camping were just two of the activities routinely enjoyed. The home was not at Coleshill but in the Vale of Evesham and opened in 1917. Dr Montessori, a pioneer in this field, is seen here at the home.

DR. MONTESSORI AND
A BESFORD BOY

In 1904 various Catholic emigration bodies amalgamated under the name of the Catholic Emigration Association. Fr Hudson personally escorted many groups of young people out to Canada to begin new lives. They stayed at the home in Ottawa until work was found for them and visits were paid afterwards to ensure their welfare. Letters from these 'old boys and girls' demonstrate the real affection they held for their former carers.

Fr Hudson's church, more formally the Church of the Sacred Heart and St Teresa, opened in 1942 as a memorial to Fr Hudson.

Fr Hudson's grave at Coleshill in the grounds of St Edward's Home. Fr James Connor, his assistant from 1915 until his untimely death from cancer in 1935, is also buried there.

St George's and St James' Homes, Coleshill, 1948.

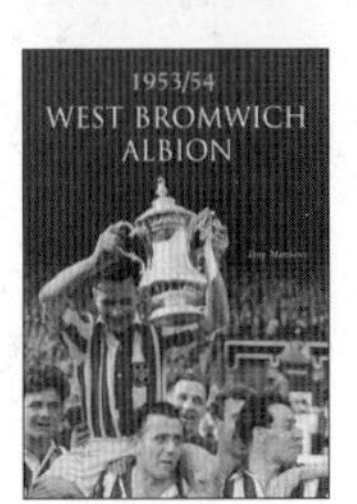

Other Birmingham titles published by Tempus

0 7524 1039 3	Acocks Green	Michael Byrne
0 7524 1808 4	Aston and Perry Barr	Maria Twist
0 7524 2767 9	Birmingham Canal Navigations	Ray Shill
0 7524 0053 3	Birmingham, Central 1870-1920	Keith Turner
0 7524 0340 0	Birmingham, Central 1920-1970	Keith Turner
0 7524 3080 7	Birmingham Cinemas	Maggie Hanson
0 7524 1862 9	Birmingham City FC	Tony Matthews
0 7524 3098 X	Birmingham Co-op	Linda & Anthony Chew
0 7524 2327 4	Birmingham: Making of the Second City	Eric Hopkins
0 7524 1809 2	Birmingham Pubs	Keith Turner
0 7524 1554 9	Birmingham Transport	Keith Turner
0 7524 1848 3	Birmingham Voices (BBC)	Helen Lloyd & Lucy Harland
0 7524 2095 X	Birmingham Women	Margaret Green
0 7524 1765 7	Boats, Smoke, Steam and Folk	Robert Davies
0 7524 2443 2	Bournville and Weoley Castle	Martin Hampson
0 7524 2475 0	Buildings of Birmingham	Peter Leather
0 7524 3041 6	Bullring	Horace Gillis
0 7524 2096 8	Castle Bromwich, Castle Vale & Shard End	Peter Drake & Marion Baxter
0 7524 1810 6	Edgbaston	Martin Hampson
0 7524 0345 1	Erdington	Marian Baxter & Peter Drake
0 7524 3057 2	Erdington Revisited	Peter Drake
0 7524 2251 0	Great Barr, Oscott and Kingstanding	Margaret Hanson & Peter Drake
0 7524 0678 7	Hall Green	Michael Byrne
0 7524 1551 4	Handsworth, Hockley and Handsworth Wood	Peter Drake
0 7524 2658 3	Harborne II	Martin Hampson
0 7524 2076 3	Heart of England Fairs	Vanessa Toulmin
0 7524 2636 2	Inner Circle: Birmingham's No. 8 Bus Route	Peter Drake
0 7524 2448 3	King Edward's School	Tony Trott
0 7524 1555 7	King's Heath	Margaret D. Green
0 7524 1052 0	King's Norton	Pauline Caswell
0 7524 2252 9	Made in Birmingham	Keith Turner
0 7524 0680 9	Moseley, Balsall Heath and Highgate	Marian Baxter & Peter Drake
0 7524 0679 5	Northfield	Pauline Caswell
0 7524 3096 3	Northfield Revisited	Martin Hampson
0 7524 0054 1	Old Harborne	Roy Clarke
0 7524 3081 5	Outer Circle: Birmingham's No. 11 Bus Route	Peter Drake
0 7524 2622 2	Quinton	Bernard Taylor
0 7524 2097 6	Rubery and the Lickey Hills, Around	Martin Hampson
0 7524 2279 0	Saltley, Duddeston and Nechells	Maria Twist
0 7524 2787 3	Seeing Birmingham by Tram	Eric Armstrong
0 7524 2635 4	Small Heath and Sparkbrook	Margaret D. Green
0 7524 1800 9	Solihull, Greater	Sue Bates
0 7524 2674 5	Stechford, Ward End and Washwood Heath	Marian Baxter
0 7524 2213 8	Sutton Coldfield 2 in 1	Marian Baxter
0 7524 2453 X	Sutton Coldfield Then & Now	Marian Baxter
0 7524 2056 9	West Bromwich Albion FC	Tony Matthews
0 7524 2224 3	West Bromwich Albion FC 100 Greats	Tony Matthews
0 7524 3049 1	Winson Green and Dudley Road	Peter Drake
0 7524 0339 7	Yardley	Michael Byrne